I0147602

The Sons
of the Farmer

The Sons of the Farmer

The continuing story of a Scottish farming family

IAIN BAIRD

THE CHOIR PRESS

Copyright © 2022 Iain Baird

All rights reserved. No part of this publication may be reproduced or transmitted in any form or by any means, electronic or mechanical including photocopying, recording or any information storage or retrieval system, without prior permission in writing from the publishers.

The right of Iain Baird to be identified as the author of this work has been asserted by him in accordance with the Copyright, Designs and Patents Act 1988

First published in the United Kingdom in 2022 by
The Choir Press

ISBN 978-1-78963-264-4

Contents

⊷⧢⊶

Introduction

～～～

John Baird and Flora Mitchell set up home at Meikle Garclaugh Farm outside New Cumnock, Ayrshire in 1866. They both came from farming families in Ayrshire and worked hard to create a thriving farm and a successful family. Over the next thirty-four years they raised six sons and two daughters, as well as many fine Ayrshire cattle that would gain an international reputation. John's sons would go on to become successful farmers and one of his sons would breed a world champion cow. Unfortunately, John would not witness this success, as he died in 1900, so it was up to Flora to shepherd her offspring through the next decades. Their story is described in my book *My Father Was a Farmer in New Cumnock*.

This book tells the stories of the sons and daughters and how they overcame adversity and celebrated successes. Inevitably there is more information regarding John and Flora's five farming sons than their two daughters. I apologise in advance for the paucity of description regarding Chrissie's life, in particular, who was a valuable daughter, wife, mother and farm worker, both at Meikle Garclaugh Farm and later at Polshill Farm. Daughter Mary's story is also very sparce.

It is the tradition in Scotland to use family names from one genera-tion to the next. Consequently, the name John, Tom and James has to be used many times to tell the story of the Baird family. Much to their annoyance, the younger members of the family usually had the name 'wee' as a prefix to their name. After elder John Baird's death in 1900, his son 'wee John' became just 'John'. Hopefully the abundance of similar names will not cause the reader too much difficulty in following which member of the family is being described. However, I have taken the liberty of changing the name of one of Barbara Stevenson's brothers from John to David, in order that the reader does not get too confused.

Being a descendant of John James Baird, or 'wee John', I have inevitably focused on my grandfather, mainly because I have been the recipient of so many stories about his life. I am grateful for my aunt Mary and other relatives who knew John James, who was able to supply me with so many accounts. Unfortunately, I was only two years old when he passed away, so have no memory of him. I have been told that he was a cheery man with a booming voice, who always had a pertinent saying for every occasion. I was told that when my mother produced her fourth son the midwife came downstairs to commiserate with my father that it was not the daughter for which he was hoping. My grandfather was quick to reassure her.

'Don't fret, lassie. If a cow keeps on having bull calves, it's not the cowman that you change, it's the bull!'

In writing this account of the sons and daughters of John and Flora Baird, I have tried to provide family and historical information in a format that is more interesting to read than just a straightforward description of a sequence of historical incidents. I have, therefore, dramatized some events with dialogues that I hope will help to depict what may have happened. I have also introduced fictional characters, mainly farmworkers and maids, but also some of the neighbouring farmers with whom John James Baird has various meetings. There is a list of the fictional characters shown for your reference. I hope, therefore, that I have also succeeded in making this book interesting for readers who are not necessarily connected with the Baird family.

I have taken every measure to try and ensure the accuracy of the historical events, however, I apologise in advance for any errors or misinterpretations. For instance, the description of Gilbert Baird's war service is based on the detailed information that was available on the Canadian Military Service Records. These records provided the dates of Gilbert's postings, as well as all the medical records of the treatment of his injuries. I give thanks to my Canadian relatives, who provided information of Hugh Baird's life in Canada, although the account of his early journey across the Atlantic and subsequent travels to McCauley are entirely speculative on my part.

I have struggled to find accurate accounts of other family events, so inevitably some of the sons and daughters of John and Flora may not have as full a description of their lives as I would have hoped. Farmers were not ones for taking many photographs of themselves or their farms, so I have not been able to add many photographs that would have enhanced the various stories and descriptions. If any members of the Baird family have any interesting and relevant photographs or documents, then I would be keen to obtain copies to add to the Baird family archives.

Iain Baird

The Baird Family at Meikle Garclaugh

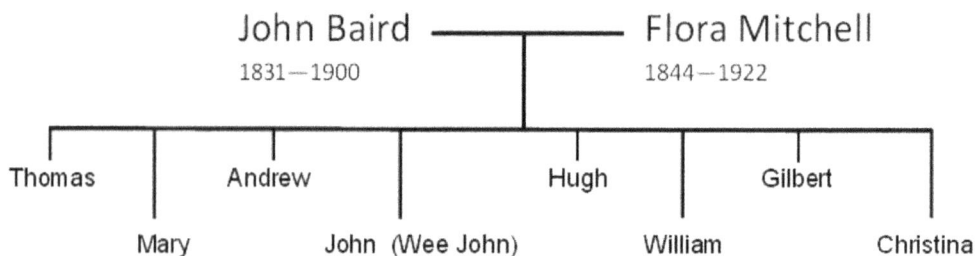

John Baird
1831—1900

Flora Mitchell
1844—1922

Thomas

Mary

Andrew

John (Wee John)

Hugh

William

Gilbert

Christina

John James Baird's family at Balladoyle

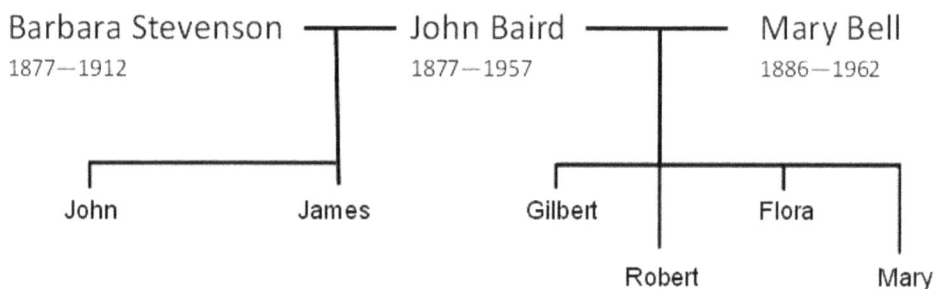

Barbara Stevenson
1877—1912

John Baird
1877—1957

Mary Bell
1886—1962

John

James

Gilbert

Robert

Flora

Mary

Hugh Baird's family in Canada

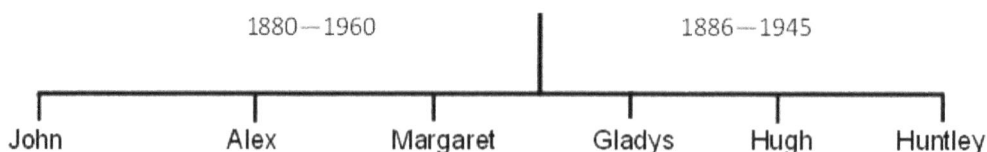

1880—1960

1886—1945

John

Alex

Margaret

Gladys

Hugh

Huntley

Gilbert Baird's family in Ayrshire

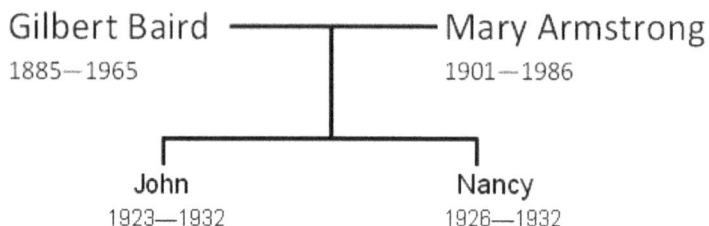

Gilbert Baird
1885—1965

Mary Armstrong
1901—1986

John
1923—1932

Nancy
1926—1932

Map of Cumberland and Southern Scotland, showing Silloth, New Cumnock and Kelso

Map of Cumberland and Southern Scotland, showing Silloth, New Cumnock and Kelso

Map of Silloth showing Balladoyle, Flagstaff and Silloth House farms

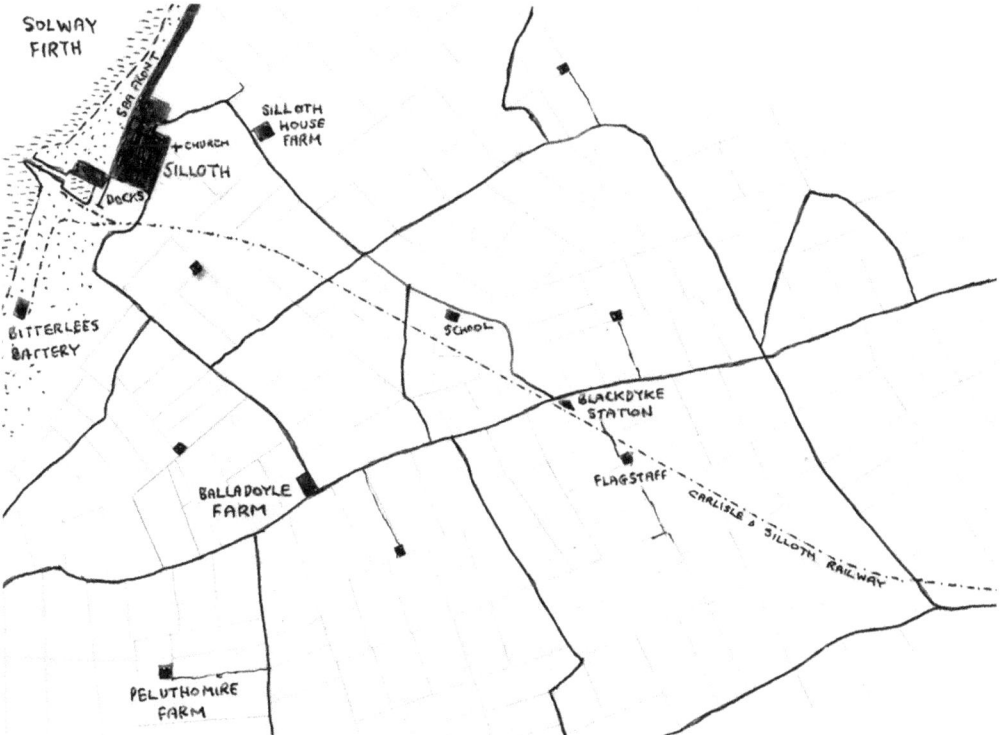

Map of Silloth showing Balladoyle, Flagstaff and Silloth House farms

Glossary of Scottish words

bairn   baby
bannock   small cake
blether   talk, gossip
braw   beautiful
break   shooting break, horse-drawn transport
breeks   trousers
byre   cattle shed
cannie   clever, wise, careful
kye   cows
doon   down
factor   estate manager
fettle   condition, vigour
fretting   worrying
ken   know
kirk   church
kye   cattle
laird   landowner of a large estate
meikle   large
mind   remember, worry
neeps   turnips
rick   large stack of hay or corn
sheugh   field drainage ditch
steading   collection of farm buildings
stooks   a small stack of sheaves of corn
twa   two
wains   children
yen   one
ye   you

CHAPTER ONE
1902

❧

It was one of those March mornings that held the promise of warmer days, but still hung on to its dank, dreik weather. The sun was starting to lighten the eastern sky but the layer of low, grey clouds was likely to stop any of its rays from warming the wet ground. John paused outside the byre door and gazed across the farmland towards the fields where he soon hoped to put out the cows to graze. The fodder was running out after a long winter and they were having to use the poor hay that was full of mould. He shivered as a cloud of mist blew down from behind the main house, in which he saw a light start to glow in a bedroom window. The Hay sisters were always up early and had lit their paraffin lamps. They were not as early risers as John though, who had already been awake for nearly an hour, even though it had not yet reached four o'clock.

'The churns are all loaded, Mr Baird,' a voice spoke from the rectangle of orange light that highlighted a door to the dairy. As if to support the statement a horse, harnessed to a milk cart next to the byre, gave a whinny and turned its head to look at John from its blinkers in anticipation. John looked towards the source of the voice to see the silhouette of a head in the dairy doorway.

'Aye, thanks, Marion. I'll be on my way,' John replied, pulling his watch from his waist coat pocket and studying the time. 'Will ye tell Jack to add some of the wheat straw to the hay. We are going to have to make the hay last a few more weeks yet,' he added.

John rubbed his hands, pulled the collar of his coat up around his neck and walked purposefully towards his next task for the morning. The milk cart squeaked and swayed as he climbed onto the seat, which was already wet from the drizzle that had started to leak from the thin clouds that shrouded the farm. As he picked up the reins the horse standing between the shafts shuffled, preparing itself to pull the cart full of heavy steel milk churns down the drive and towards the track that would lead to Kilmaurs Station. Here the seventeen-gallon conical churns of milk would join those from other farms, to be taken up the railway line to Glasgow. The Glasgow train would steam out of Kilmaurs Station at quarter to five in the morning, which was why John woke at three o'clock to get the milking completed in time.

After a winter of deep snow and icy winds there were many holes in the main road to Kilmaurs, as well as on the track that led to Mid-Buiston Farm, where John had started as the manager for the Hay sisters the year before. He had left the family farm at New Cumnock, where he had been born and grew up, soon after his father had passed on. As the third son of six boys, he knew that he would have to find his own way in the farming world. But it wasn't just his position in the family hierarchy that led him to this position as farm manager, it was a burning desire to prove to himself and his fiancé that he could prosper as a farmer.

The road to Kilmaurs ran close to the railway line, so after unloading the churns of milk at the station and collecting the empty ones from the previous day, he watched the clouds of steam and ash issue from the engine as it headed north towards Stewarton, its next stop on the way to Glasgow. The noise of the train of wagons on the iron rails made John aware of the rumblings in his stomach. His thoughts turned to the hot porridge that he hoped would be waiting on the breakfast table when he got back to the house. He arrived back into the yard in front of the two-storey farmhouse that formed the northern side of an open square of buildings. He climbed down from the cart and stretched his back and looked around for his labourer, Jack Vass. He was nowhere in sight so John shouted his name and waited for some response, but all that he could hear was the occasional cough from the cattle in their sheds.

'Vass, where are ye?' John shouted again. He heard the scrape of boots on the flagstones in the byre then a small man appeared through the doorway.

'Aye, Mr Baird. Don't fret, I was just on my way,' Jack Vass replied in his usual unconcerned and disrespectful manner.

'Just gie the horse some feed then take some neeps around to the sheep in the back meadow.' He found himself speaking to Jack's back as he was already leading the horse and cart away towards the horse boxes. Jack had been working at Mid-Buiston Farm for many years and John could not understand why the Hay sisters had kept him on for so long, as he always seemed to find an excuse to avoid hard work. He would need to speak to the sisters about getting another hand at the next hiring fair. His stomach gave another rumble, so he turned and made his way to the back door of the main house.

The Hay sisters had been born on the farm and had lived with their parents and their siblings. Their eldest brother, James, had been expected to take over the farm, but he had died suddenly, which was why they needed a manager to run the farm. The second son had emigrated to New Zealand, while the third son had also left the farm many years previously to find his own way in the world. Agnes and Jeanie had tried to keep the farm going since James' death, but they needed someone who they could trust to oversee the work and ensure that the farm was being properly managed. They took on John Baird as manager, a young man of only twenty-three, as the reputation of the Ayrshire herd at Meikle Garclaugh Farm was well known, even here, forty miles to the north. When he came up to meet the two sisters they were immediately taken by his determined manner and, if truth be known, his good looks.

John hung his coat in the back place then unlaced and removed his boots. He could hear the clatter of activity in the kitchen next door and felt the warmth of the range as he entered.

'Good marning, Mr Baird,' May, one of the housemaids, greeted him.

'Good marning to you, May. Are the sisters up yet?' John replied.

'Aye, Marion has just taken some water up to them, so they won't be lang.'

May was the younger of the two maids who looked after the house and tended to the needs of Agnes and Jeanie Hay. Marion also helped out in the dairy.

John spotted some cheese on the kitchen table and he moved across to cut himself a good-sized piece.

'Ahh, Mr Baird, you know that Miss Agnes will want to know why the cheese is smaller than it was last night,' May pleaded.

John paused with his knife above the cheese, then looked at May and smiled.

'Aye, I widnae want ye to get into trouble. I'll wait for the breakfast to be served. Let's hope that it won't be lang.'

John felt his stomach rumble again, so he went into the back place where he knew there was a bag of carrots and helped himself to one. Agnes and Jean Hay came down from their room a little while later. John was already seated at the breakfast table and he stood up as they entered.

'Good morning, John,' Agnes greeted him. 'It's another driek day I see.'

'Well, you will be off to yer friend's wedding today, John?' enquired Jean, as she took her usual place at the table.

'Aye, I will make sure that Jack kens what jobs need to be done, then I will get him to take me doon to the station. I'll be back for the milking this afternoon,' John replied.

'You'll give our regards to yer mither, will ye, John?' asked Agnes.

'Aye, I will pass on yer greetings,' John responded, but his attention was taken by the bowl of porridge that May had brought through from the kitchen. He was starting to feel very hungry, but knew that the sisters would be served first. Thankfully May was well used to John's desire for food and quickly served the sisters before giving John his breakfast. The Hay sisters were quite petite and did not have large appetites. They therefore did not understand the need for a healthy man to eat large portions. This was made worse by their constant monitoring of the food that was in the house, making it difficult for John to supplement his meagre portions by helping himself to food from the larder, like he used to do when he was at home.

**

The clouds were starting to clear as Jack Vass took John to Stewarton station in the milk cart. The farm had a gig that the sisters used, but John was in a hurry to catch the nine o'clock Glasgow and South Western express train, which would head south towards Dumfries, so did not want to waste the time getting the horse hitched up to the gig. He gave instructions for Jack to collect him at three o'clock in the afternoon.

The express train stopped at Kilmarnock and then sped on towards the coalfields around Cumnock, where it was due to stop once more before Dumfries. John left the train here, as it was not due to stop at New Cumnock, his destination. He would have to wait at Cumnock station for a slower train to take the last few miles. As impatient as ever, he paced the station platform and looked at his pocket watch once more.

'Don't worry, sir, it is not often late. I am sure that you will be on time for your meeting.' A voice spoke to John from behind. He turned to see the smiling face of the station master.

'Meeting?' John replied, looking somewhat surprised.

'Well sir, the way that ye've been pacing the platform it is clear that ye're keen to get on your way, so it must be an important meeting that awaits ye.' The station master chuckled.

John returned the chuckle. 'Aye. I'm off to a friend's wedding. I dinnae want to be late.'

John did not mention that although he was keen to meet up with his family, he was also keen to see his fiancé, Barbara Stevenson. Barbara lived at Nether Cairn, a farm on the opposite side of the River Nith to his boyhood home, Meikle Garclaugh Farm. He would ask his brother Andrew if he could borrow one of the farm's horses and cross the river through the ford at the bottom of the fields, in order to reach Nether Cairn. His musings were interrupted by the arrival of the train for which he had been waiting. The station master had left him and approached the edge of the platform as it slowed and squealed to a stop in a cloud of white steam that drifted towards John. John could smell the soot and oil, which brought back memories from his childhood when the smoke from the trains drifted across the fields as they rattled down the main line that crossed Meikle Garclaugh Farm.

The train was soon on its way and passing the small lochs outside New Cumnock, where it slowed to discharge its passengers. Deposited on the platform, John walked briskly past the ticket office to get a taxi gig to the farm. As the gig made its way along the Mansfield road, he studied the fields that lay on either side and gave a judgemental inspection of the cattle that were grazing. An activity known as 'hedge farming' and common amongst all farmers, as they secretly compared their own crops and livestock to those of other famers.

The gig passed the estate house at Mansfield and rattled down the short track to the yard at Meikle Garclaugh. John paid the driver, leapt out of the gig and strode into the farm house, where he was greeted by his mother and little sister Chrissie.

Chrissie ran up to John and gave him a big hug. 'Hello there, John. It's guid to see yer agin.'

'Well, that's a grand welcome, Chrissie. It's guid to see you as well,' John responded.

Flora, John's mother, was more restrained. 'I suppose yer'll be wanting some lunch Ye dinnae look as if ye hae been eating much,' she greeted him.

'There will be some food at the wedding, Mither, but I'll grab some bread and cheese now, as it's bin a while since breakfast,' John replied.

Flora smiled. She was well used to the large appetites of her sons. 'Aye, well help yourself, ye usually do.'

As John tucked into a large slice of bread topped with Dunlop cheese from the Garclaugh dairy, his mother filled him in with news of his siblings.

'Well Tom and Elizabeth are settled in at Birnieknowe Farm. They will have a lot of work to do to get the farm sorted and it's rough grazing up there on that hill. At least Elizabeth kens the farm, having been a dairymaid there for so lang.' She paused while John put a large chunk of bread into his mouth and then she continued with news of John's other brother. 'Andrew is doing fine with all the kye. He hopes to show one of his bulls in the Highland Show in the summer. His anaemia is getting worse though and he often has to have a lie down in the afternoons. Mary now helps out in the byre with Andrew.'

She paused again as John helped himself to yet more bread and cheese.

Tom was John's eldest brother. It was expected that he would take over the tenancy of Garclaugh, but he went to work for a while at his uncle's farm at Back Rogerton and met Elizabeth, who was working at the neighbouring farm of Birnieknowe. John Begg, who farmed Birnieknowe, offered the tenancy to Tom, as he had no sons to inherit the farm. It was difficult to tell which held the greatest attraction for Tom: the tenancy of a farm or the attractive dairymaid. It was probably the latter.

Flora continued with her news of John's younger brothers.

'Hugh is still determined to gae off to Canada. I've lent him the money for his passage. There is a ship leaving in May, which he intends to take. The government are offering land at a very cheap price. I'm surprised that you hav'nae thought about joining him.'

'Aye. I hae thought about it. Perhaps I'll wait and see how things work out for Hugh,' John responded.

'Gilbert's doing a grand job around the farm. He's a dab hand with the horses and the plough. Tom has taught him well. And then there's Will.' Flora's voice trailed off.

William was born severely handicapped and although aware of his surroundings and his family members, he was not capable of even feeding himself. He spent much of the day in a wooden pen that had been constructed to stop him crawling towards places where he could hurt himself or break things. He has seventeen now and no longer a boy.

'Mary does a lot of the caring of Will and we have a new maid, Sarah Coe, who is very sensible. Mary is a grand help around the house although she still has her sombre times. I've been keeping her busy with jobs, to distract her a wee bit.'

'That hasn't changed much then, Maw!', John replied with a smile.

Some years ago, John's sister Mary woke from the anaesthetic during an operation in hospital. As a result of this trauma, she still suffered with severe bouts of depression and panic attacks.

'Then there's wee Chrissie, who is a grand help in the kitchen.' Flora stopped and looked at John as he lent back in his chair, his hunger satisfied.

'So, will ye be going straight back to Mid-Buiston after the wedding?'

'I need to get back for the milking, so I'll need to go straight to the station. I'll hae a walk oot around the farm to see Hugh and Gilbert now though,' John replied.

John left Flora in the dining room and made his way out of the house. He was in his best clothes so did not want to get them dirty by going into the byre and walking on the muddy tracks. He carefully walked across the yard and put his head into one of the stables, where he heard the sound of someone working. He found Hugh putting some hay into nets for the horses.

'Ye still got plenty of guid hay then.' John's voice boomed into the stable.

Hugh and the horses flinched at the sudden loud voice.

'Saints preserve us, John, ye gave me a fright,' Hugh responded. 'Fancy creeping up on a fella like that.'

John laughed. 'It's good to see ye, Hugh. I hear ye've at last made plans for Canada.'

'Aye, I'll be shipping oot on the thirteenth of May from Liverpool,' Hugh replied. 'I'm excited and I'm nervous.'

'Maw will miss ye aboot the farm. She might have to get another hand in to help Andrew, although I hear that Gilbert is proving himself useful.'

'Aye, but there's plenty of men looking for work, I'm sure they will get someone,' Hugh added.

'Hae ye been ower to Birnieknowe since Tom took it ower? I thought that there may be a wee attraction for ye there.' John chuckled.

Hugh had been courting a young woman called Margaret Corbett, whose family lived in a cottage at Birnieknowe. Hugh met her when he visited the farm with his brother Tom. Tom's wife, Elizabeth Hamilton, worked at Birnieknowe as a dairymaid, while Margaret worked in the farmhouse of her uncle, John Begg and his wife. Now Hugh was keen to persuade Margaret Corbett to be his wife. However, he declined to rise to his brother's teasing and just smiled back to him.

Seeing that he wasn't going to get a response from his brother, John continued. 'Aye well, I'll come ower afore ye take ship. It'll be quite an adventure; ye'll hae to write to us when ye get there.'

'I'll be going oot for a year or twa first to see what it is like. If I get offered some good farmland, I will come back ower to get some cattle and horses. Maw says that she will loan me some money,' Hugh explained.

'I hope that there will be enough left ower after Tom has taken his chunk of the inheritance. He seems to think that as he is the elder brother that he is entitled to a larger share,' John replied with more than a touch of annoyance.

'Maw says that she will see me right, so I can't imagine that Tom will stand up to Mither.'

'No, yer right there. Anyway, I'm going to catch up with Gilbert and Mary, then I'll be off to Nether Cairn for the wedding,' John noted, as he left Hugh to finish sorting the Clydesdale horses in the stables.

*****

The sun was starting to disperse the clouds as John made his way on the borrowed horse towards the River Nith and on to Nether Cairn. At the bottom of the river meadows at Garclaugh was a ford that could be used if the river was not too high. John stopped his horse at the river's edge and surveyed the river. It was higher than he would have liked, but he knew the horse and it was steady and careful. He urged it forwards towards the current and lifted his feet out of the stirrups so that they did not get wet. The horse placed its large hairy feet into the water and strode forwards. Clydesdale horses were strong and reliable. They were used throughout Scotland for work on the farm, as they were not as large as the English shire horses and were ideal for the smaller fields found in Scotland. The Clydesdale that John had saddled up was one that had been bred on the farm, so John knew it well from when it was a foal. He trusted it and it trusted John, so when John urged it into the river, it responded immediately and waded confidently through the fast current. John was relieved, however, when it finally climbed up the slope on the far side and he was able to lower his legs and put his feet back into the stirrups. He soon reached the main road from New Cumnock to Kirkconnel. The large imposing hill called The Knipe was to his right. Nether Cairn Farm was positioned at the base of the hill, nestled into a flat area just off the main road. The main house looked out at the road, so as John walked the horse down the drive, he could see members of the Stevenson family in the garden enjoying the sunshine that had now broken out of its cloudy confines. One of the group spotted him and walked quickly over to the wall to greet him. It was his fiancée, Barbara. He felt his heart beat faster and his stomach turned.

'Hello, John. I was hoping that ye would have been able to get here sooner. I've missed ye. Take the horse round to the stables, ye'll see the gig that Mungo has brought over. Ye can tie yer horse to the wall next to it,' Barbara instructed.

John walked his horse along the track that led alongside the farmhouse towards the steading. At the end of the track were a cluster of buildings, both to the right and left, but the stables were almost opposite so John tied up his horse with a net of hay for its lunch. Mungo Sloan was a school friend of John and it was his wedding to Barbara's sister Janet, or Jessie as most folk called her, that was taking place this day. As with all famers, the wedding was timed to fit between the morning and the afternoon milking, although Mungo had been relieved this duty for the day.

As John joined the group at the front of the house he was welcomed by Barbara's father James and her brother Allan. Most of the Stevenson ladies were all upstairs helping to get Jessie ready for the wedding or in the kitchen preparing food.

Mungo came across and took John's outstretched hand.

'Thanks for getting here in time, John. I was worried that ye widnae be here for the service.'

'It's nae bother, Mungo. I've to catch the train by quarter to three, so it gives me plenty of time during the day. I may hae to have a wee snooze at some stage though, but I will try to keep my eyes open during the service. I dinnae want ye marrying the wrong Stevenson daughter.' John laughed.

The minister arrived at the allotted time and the service took place in the front room of the farmhouse, so space was restricted. The ladies had been given chairs at the front of the room, while the men folk stood shoulder to shoulder at the back. The minister rattled through the service and the vows were made, to a smattering of cheers and applause from the crowded room. This was followed by a meal prepared by Barbara's mother Annie, Barbara and the maid. It gave John an opportunity to satisfy his appetite once more. He had hardly spoken to Barbara as she was so busy in the kitchen, so he was pleased when she appeared at the doorway and gave him one her glorious smiles. Mungo noticed the exchange and announced in a loud voice.

'Aye, well it looks as if there will be another wedding soon. When are ye twa going to fix a date?'

Barbara giggled and disappeared back into the kitchen, leaving John to respond to Mungo and the looks of everyone in the room.

'When I have got my ain farm. I don't intend to be managing someone else's farm for much longer,' John asserted.

This response was met with nods of approval from the elder guests and in particular by Barbara's father.

The wedding meal came to an end. John and Barbara had found time to meet and even exchange quick kisses. Mungo and Jessie had left for their honeymoon at a local hotel and guests had started to leave. John looked at his watch and realised that he too would have to make his way back to the station. He made his farewells to the Stevensons and walked back to his horse with Barbara.

'How lang will it be for ye to get yer ain farm, John?'

'As soon as I have enough money to set up a farm. There's no point in taking on a tenancy unless I can buy the stock,' John explained. He too was keen for their marriage to take place, but wanted to do things in the proper order.

Barbara paused thoughtfully. 'Aye, yer right.' She then gave him a peck on the lips and skipped away into the house to help tidy up after the wedding.

'I'll see ye soon,' she shouted at John and waved as she disappeared into the back door of the kitchen.

'As soon as possible,' John muttered to himself and then hauled himself up into the saddle of his horse.

John arrived back at Mid-Buiston in time to help with the end of the milking. The milk cows were in their stalls in the byre and Marion was sitting on her three-legged stool with her head leaning against one of the cows, with her hands steadily squeezing milk from the udder. There were no machines at this time; all the cows had to be hand milked, which was back-breaking and tedious work. At least they did not make any cheese on the farm, so a full-time dairy maid was not needed. It was dark by the time they had got all the work done and they were all keen to get some supper and sleep. John would still have some book work to do after supper, despite another early start to next day, so it would be a while before he was able to put his head on a pillow.

***

The steamship Sardinian left Glasgow docks on 13 May bound for Montreal in Canada. On board was a twenty-two-year-old Hugh Baird,

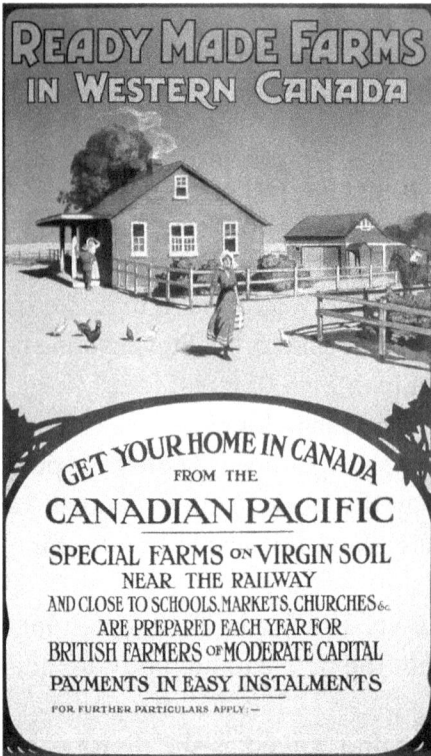

venturing abroad to seek a new life in the colonies. The British government had been advertising for farmers to travel to Canada, as well as Australia and New Zealand, and had been offering 160 acres of arable land for free. Posters and magazines showed pictures of bountiful farms with well-fed cattle and horses, golden fields of wheat and one showed a handsome husband and wife standing in front of a flower-bedecked farmhouse. Hugh was keen to emigrate to Canada and wanted to have his share of this land of 'milk and honey'.

The voyage across to Montreal took seven days. Fortunately, the sea was fairly calm, or at least as calm as the north Atlantic permits. The ship had many individuals and families who were also travelling to find a new life; most, like Hugh, having never been on a ship before. It was clear that many of the passengers were not from Britain and Hugh heard a variety of languages that he could not identify. Hugh shared a small cabin with a young Glaswegian man called Jim, who hoped to find work that did not involve long shifts down a coal mine. They shared their stories and their hopes for the future. When the ship reached Montreal, they were firm friends and had decided to stay together for this adventure. In the meantime they spent time on the decks watching the large waves roll past the ship, making the steel plates in the hull groan and judder. As the ship approached Canada the air temperature dropped dramatically and snow fell from large black clouds that blew down from the North Pole. They could see large icebergs in the distance that the crew watched with suspicion. Eventually they spotted land and it seemed that the ship was headed straight into it, but splitting the land was the Gulf of St Lawrence, into which

Montreal Harbour around 1910

they steamed. It gave them shelter from the wind and rough seas of the north Atlantic. Hugh and Jim studied the forested hills that back-dropped the journey to Quebec and the St Lawrence River. Eventually, they reached Montreal and the ship berthed to allow its passengers to disembark.

The scene around the docks was a noisy confusion of porters, disembarking passengers and trolleys laden with suitcases and crates. Hugh and Jim just had kitbags, which they could carry on their shoulders, so they could make their way through the crowds easily. Hugh had the name of a government office that would provide advice and directions. After a few enquiries they found the correct office and the long queue that stretched out onto the pavement. They took their places and shuffled slowly towards the grand steps of the colonial building, which was called the Immigration Hall. Eventually after an hour of so they reached the desk of a clerk who took their names and issued them with a form to complete and present at another immigration hall when they reached their destination. Their destination was to be the town of Austin in Manitoba, right in the middle of the prairies. Hugh and Jim then found lodgings for the night, after purchasing train tickets for their long journey the next day.

The Canadian Pacific Railway station in Montreal was as noisy and crowded as the docks the previous day. Like Hugh and Jim, there were many passengers heading west to find a new life. The journey would take three days, so the train had sleeper carriages with three tiers of bunk beds along each side. Privacy was provided by a short curtain that could be pulled across the side of the bed. During the day passengers could sit in carriages that had large windows, from which Hugh and Jim marvelled at the scenery. Much of the landscape from Montreal reminded Hugh of the West of Scotland, with rolling hills covered in forest. While travelling through an area of bushes and grass Hugh remarked to one of the crew that the cattle that he could see looked very different to those in Scotland. Hugh was amazed to be told that the animals that he could see were bears, not cattle.

After a stop at Fort William, where they were able to view the largest fresh water lake in the world, Lake Superior, the train headed further west towards the town of Winnipeg. The forest started to thin out and the land looked more like the prairie that Hugh has read about in his preparation for the journey. Hugh and Jim were expecting to see wild rampaging Indians, but they were disappointed to see none.

The journey to Winnipeg passed through a region dotted with many lakes, both large and small. There were many bridges and cuttings along this stretch of the railway, the bridges being constructed of thousands of long logs bolted together. In fact, everything seemed to depend on trees, even the locomotive that belched black smoke across the landscape. By the time that they reached Winnipeg Hugh and Jim had become tired of the train and the cramped conditions. Jim had commented that working at a coalface had more space than their sleeping carriage.

Many of the passengers left the train at Winnipeg, and Hugh and Jim joined them. They found the immigration hall and took a meal that was available, before settling down to a more comfortable night on the beds that were also provided. Immigration Halls provided accommodation for about two hundred people and were provided by the government to avoid immigrants being conned out of their savings by unscrupulous traders. As well as hot meals and sleeping rooms, they also gave out advice to immigrants about where to apply for free farmland. Hugh met with one of the officials who told Hugh that if he had the money then he should try and buy some land, as the free land was often poor scrubland far from water.

The next day Hugh set out on his own for Austin, Jim having decided to stay in Winnipeg to find work as a labourer. They had wished each other well on each other's futures. It was a fairly short train journey from Winnipeg to Austin, where Hugh had been advised to search for land to purchase. He found lodgings in a small immigration hall, where there was hardly an English word to be heard. It seemed that every country in Europe had sent a family west to Canada. He offered himself to work at the immigration hall, but it was not long before his working abilities were spotted and he was offered some paid labouring work. He used his time and his earnings to find more suitable lodgings and it was not long before he heard some familiar Scottish voices and introduced himself to a group of fellow Scots who were working nearby. Over a meal at a nearby restaurant he was advised to travel further west to the town of McAuley where there was a settlement of Scots and where there was good land for sale. So, his journey west continued until he finally left the train at the small settlement of McAuley. As the train pulled away, he looked around him at the flat landscape that stretched to the horizon without a hill in sight. It was certainly not Ayrshire. The town was barely a town, with only a collection of wooden single-storey houses alongside the railway line itself. One of them advertised itself as a hotel so he made his way to it, wondering if he had made the right decision.

The hotel proved to be the focal point of the town, with many locals calling in for beer or for a meal. Through his conversations with these visitors, he met up with the land agent and was soon visiting plots of land in the area that were for sale. He eventually settled on one large plot and shook hands on the purchase. He had at last started on his new life in Canada. Now he had to make it a home suitable for a wife.

***

It had been eighteen months since Britain had mourned the death of Queen Victoria. She had been Britain's longest reigning monarch and the majority of British citizens had only ever known her as their queen. In some ways it was fitting that she should pass away when she did, leaving her eldest son to begin the Edwardian era three weeks into a new century. Despite the death of Queen Victoria being far from an unexpected event, the planning of the coronation of King Edward VII took until August of that year. In New Cumnock, as in all the towns, the bunting had been displayed and street parties to celebrate the coronation were planned. The weather, however, was one factor that the town council could not plan, and, so far, the year had been cold and wet. John had come over from Mid-Buiston for the day and was enjoying the coronation festivities with Barbara and members of her family. As they stood watching the parade Mungo Sloan and his new wife, Jessie, joined them.

'Good morning, Mrs Stevenson, hello, Barbara and John. I hope that you are all well,' Mungo enquired, while Jessie hugged her mother and Barbara.

'Aye, we're in good fettle. How are things over at Castlemains Farm?' John replied.

'Aye. Everyone is doing well. We could do we some drier weather, like everyone else, but we're all well,' Mungo replied. 'Are you waiting to see anyone in the parade?'

'Aye. Wee Mary is on the kirk float. They are all dressed up to look like angels. We even made her some wings to wear,' Barbara explained. 'She was so excited to be chosen to be on the float.'

Mary was Barbara's niece, by her eldest brother James. Mary's mother died soon after she was born, so she now spends most of her time at Nether Cairn. As the youngest in the family Barbara enjoyed being an elder 'sister' to Mary.

'There she is, there she is,' Barbara shouted, jumping up and down with excitement.

John and Mungo looked at each other, then burst out laughing.

'I think that ye might be getting a wee bit too excited Barbara,' Jessie said quietly to her sister. Barbara immediately stopped jumping, smoothed down her dress and looked down at the ground, a little embarrassed.

'If ye want to get excited, Barbara, ye get excited. Don't let Jessie spoil yer fun.' John chuckled at his fiancé. He studied Barbara, this bundle of fun and feminine charm, and felt his love for her make him glow inside. They had first met when they were children. It was an inauspicious first meeting when John had accidently fallen into the muck in a calf pen. His musings were interrupted by the arrival of the kirk float in front of them. Barbara could not contain her excitement any longer and despite her sister's previous admonishment she waved frantically at wee Mary on the float.

Their attention was later taken by an unfamiliar noise and the appearance of a motor car in the parade. It rattled and sputtered and gave the occasional pop that frightened a pair of horses pulling a display wagon behind.

'What a strange machine,' Barbara exclaimed.

'It's the future,' John responded.

'The future? How's that going to replace a horse?' Mungo added. 'A horse can go doon a road, across a field, jump over hedges and wade through a river. I would like to see that machine do all those.'

'Aye, but they will develop these motor cars more and when roads get better made, then you will be able to go much faster than a horse. You wait and see,' John replied.

There was a general muttering in the crowd and it was clear than many people agreed with Mungo, but others felt the same as John. It certainly attracted the attention of the boys in the crowd, who followed it down the road, shouting at the driver to give them a ride. The discussion on the future of motor cars was broken by an announcement from James.

'I had a letter from oor David.' He then looked at John and Mungo before adding further explanation. 'David is my wee brother. He's working down in London.'

'Aye, he works in a bank,' Barbara added.

'He's a lang way from hame,' Mungo asked. 'Does he no miss his family?'

'He lives with his cousin and her husband, who works in the same bank, so he has some family around. But it was grand to receive a letter with all his news,' James responded. 'He sounds as if he is enjoying life in a big city and from what he was saying he is doing well down there. He hopes to come up to visit us in September.'

'Oh, that will be grand,' Barbara exclaimed in her usually vivacious manner.

The coronation parade had now passed and the townsfolk started to disperse to various tea parties that were taking place in halls and hotels. John announced that he would need to get the train back to Kilmaurs, in order to get the milking started, while Mungo and James said the same. The cows don't stop producing milk even for the coronation of a new king.

That evening bonfires were lit at the top of Corsecon and Blackcraig hill, though the mist came down and hid them from the crowds that had gathered by the side of the River Afton to see the orange flames. But the children had had an exciting day and had the chance to taste cakes and sweets that were not available normally. The Edwardian era had begun.

CHAPTER 2

1903

ᖇᕦᕤᖆ

Hugh had purchased land in Canada and now needed to make it into a farm. He was determined to stock the farm with the best cattle and horses that he could find and there was only one place where he would find them, and that was in his home town of New Cumnock. He was soon taking a ship back across to Canada, having purchased two Clydesdale horses, a mare and a stallion, six Ayrshire cows and one of his brother's Ayrshire bulls. These were all loaded onto the ship *Sardinian* and they left Glasgow on the 2 May.

He was now familiar with the crossing and did not need to fill his days on the ship staring at the rolling waves. He decided to use the time to write a poem about his journey for the woman that he had asked to be his wife, Margaret Scott. He titled his poem:

An Emigrant's Journey to Canada

'Twas an early day in May
In nineteen hundred and three
I bade farewell to the home of my birth
To cross the briny sea.

With many a tear and fond word
I took myself away
To see what fortune had in store
Beyond the tossing frae.

On second May we did set sail
Upon the ship Sardinian
Five hundred emigrants her freight
All bound for the Dominion.

As down the Clyde we gently sailed
Into the busy firth
Full many a man shed tears to leave
The land that gave him birth.

Then through the Irish Channel
Out to the swollen deep
The passengers retired to rest
But few to have sound sleep.

The bed was very comfy
The grub was plenty enough
The coffee was unsavoury
The meat was ought but tough.

We woke next morning early
Upon the raging main
I was not sick, but thought
I'd never see land again.

Two days upon the water
Without the sight of land
The rolling waves around us
This cheerful, happy band.

The third day, in the distance
A little speck we spied
On to it crept 'till clear in view
'A ship,' the crew all cried.

Next morning at the dawning
We found this ship abreast,
Her motion power was greater
And so she proved the best.

She crossed our bows at midday
And sailing duly west
Our prayer, "God save the cargo
And may you truly trust."

For two more days we sailed away
Amid the toss and tumble
The storage oft' times found cause
To grumble, grumble, grumble.

A bird upon the water
The only sign of life
Sent by the great Creator
To wean from sinful strife.

Now all who are despondent
Here is a chance once more
Forgetting things behind
And proving things before.

At three o'clock on Saturday
We saw on our port side
Two great monster icebergs
Afloating with the tide.

As round Cape Race we ploughed our way
On Sunday morning early
Newfoundland's coast was clear in view
The snow-clad hills show clearly.

Then passed two Frenchy islands
Into the gulf at St Lawrence
The ragged coast seemed cold and bare
And had a bleak appearance

When first we saw Canadian soil
It did look a treat
The bonny hills were clad with snow
The wood and valleys sweet.

Then passed Cape Gas, that point of land
That just into the river
The St Lawrence banks a lovely sight
A sight to remember ever.'

Hugh Baird 17ᵗʰ May 1903.

During the crossing Hugh checked on the welfare of his animals. They were strapped tightly into stalls, clearly uneasy with the manner in which the floor sometimes moved, making them stagger to keep their balance. These beasts were valuable, beyond what he paid for them, and Hugh was pleased when they reached Montreal and he was able to unload them. He watched as each animal was hoisted by crane in a canvas sling. Some of them kicked their legs and were trying to get out of the sling, but thankfully none succeeded. They were soon all tethered on the dockside, before being led through the streets to the railway terminal. Here they would spend the night in large pens before being loaded onto a train the next morning for their long journey to McCauley.

***

Back at Meikle Garclaugh Farm in Ayrshire, Hugh's brother Andrew was also moving some of his cattle into pens, ready for the coming shows at which he hoped to win some awards. As well as the prestige of winning, awards would also bring in buyers from across the world. One of his cows, Garclaugh Spottie, had won accolades in America for the amount of milk that it was producing. Ayrshire cattle were valued by farmers in the colonies and in the United States, as they could perform well even with the rough grazing that characterised the newly developed farms on the prairies. Andrew was one of several farmers in the district who were breeding excellent cows and bulls. The Garclaugh herd was now well known in Canada and Andrew was pleased to provide Hugh with some breeding stock that would create more interest in Canadian farms.

As the railways had allowed fresh milk to be delivered to the centre of cities such as Glasgow, there had also been a huge increase in the incidence of tuberculosis amongst the population. Some doctors had linked the tuberculosis in their patients to the tuberculosis seen in cattle and had blamed the milk from these infected cows as the source of human tuberculosis. The Royal Highland Agricultural Society of Scotland had recently published reports of research that had been done showing that bovine tuberculosis was a different strain of bacteria to human tuberculosis and that it was not possible for people to catch the disease from milk from infected cattle. Other evidence, however, suggested that there was a link and there was pressure to try and remove infected cows from herds. Because tuberculosis can take a long time to develop, it is not always easy to establish when a person might have become infected, so establishing a causal link would be difficult. So, as well as producing top quality breeding cattle, Andrew was also keen that their dairy would be recognised as producing top quality milk and cheese.

Andrew had been suffering from a variety of medical symptoms for some years. They had been getting worse more recently and he had been diagnosed with pernicious anaemia. The family doctor, Richard Richardson, had suggested a number of treatments to help alleviate the symptoms, including eating raw liver, but his symptoms had only got worse. He was having to take frequent rests during the day when the fatigue became overwhelming. Thankfully he had Gilbert to help out on the farm with the heavy work, as well as other good farmhands. Andrew's skill at breeding was in the good eye that he had for cows and bulls that he selected for cross-breeding, so his affliction did not hamper his work with the cattle too much.

It was yet another wet day during a particularly wet summer. Andrew shook his coat of rain water, hung it in the back place of the farmhouse at Garclaugh and went through to the kitchen, where his mother, Flora, was busy making a pie for supper.

'Be cannie round the table, there's flour on the top,' she warned. Flora was now the mistress and master of the Garclaugh household and made sure that everyone knew.

'Aye, I will,' Andrew responded quietly.

'I heard today that your Uncle James has passed on. There's been a fair few of deaths up at Blairkip recently. There was Helen, who died during one of her epileptic fits, back two year ago now. Then your cousin Tom. It doesn't seem lang ago that we were all enjoying his wedding at Sorn Castle, and now James.' Flora paused in thought, then continued. 'Perhaps this new sanatorium that they are building will help to treat folk that are ill. It's about time that we had a hospital in the town.'

Andrew appeared to be only half-listening to what his mother was telling him.

'Are you listening, Andrew?' Flora asked in an admonishing tone.

'Aye, I'm listening, mither. Ye were telling me how the Baird family is all dying off.' Andrew responded.

'Och, I'm no saying that at all. For every death, there's a birth, as your brother Tom and Elizabeth have shown. I wonder how their wee bairn John is getting on? I hav'nae heard any news from them for a while. Perhaps you or Gilbert could take me ower to Birnieknowe in the gig one day?' Flora asked.

'Aye I am sure that Gilbert would be happy to take the gig oot,' Andrew replied.

'I hear that Barbara's mither is no so well either,' Flora continued.

'Who?' Andrew replied

'Barbara Stevenson's mither, Annie. Yer brother John's future mither-in-law,' Flora emphasised.

'Oh. Aye,' Andrew replied wearily.

'Perhaps ye should have a lie doon, Andrew? Ye look tired,' Flora said more sympathetically.

'Aye. I think I will,' Andrew replied, as he shuffled off to the living room to sit in his faither's chair.

Like Andrew's health the weather that year did not improve. October was particularly wet, without a single dry day. The potato harvest was ruined and any hope of harvesting the late corn was washed away. Up at Mid-Buiston John was struggling in the mud. He was trying to keep the cows in the meadows for as long as possible, as they had not been able to make much good hay that summer. The farm had a thick bed of clay that turned to a glutinous quagmire, making it very difficult for the cows to walk through the gateways. When they did reach the byre, their udders were covered in mud and it took a long time to clean the teats so that they could be milked. The time taken to milk the herd had increased considerably. John had missed the milk train one morning and had to try and sell the milk from door to door in Kilmaurs, much to the fury of the normal milk man who supplied the homes.

John was standing in the gateway to a field in the valley behind the steading. Jack Vass came plodding through the mud towards him.

'It looks as if we have a loch forming over there, Jack,' John said, pointing to the water that was accumulating in the hollow.

'Aye. Well that's where the old loch used to be, Mr Baird, it usually comes back in wet years.'

'Old loch? What do you mean?'

'Aye Buiston Loch used to be a muckle affair. Back in the old days they drained a lot of this valley and the loch disappeared. It had a wee island in the middle that was called Swan Knowe, due to the swans that used to nest on it. Anyhow when they drained the loch they found lots of log beams. The farmer here carted the logs away and used them for building sheds.' Jack paused, but could see that John was interested in the story of Loch Buiston, so he continued.

'Anyhow, aboot twenty year ago some archaeologist chap came over and dug into it and found all sorts of stuff. It turned oot that there was some sort of hame built in the middle of the loch, and the island was the remains of it. I think they called it a crannog. A lot of the things that they found are in the national museum in Edinburgh. Aye, Buiston became famous for a while. They even found a boat and not a wee yen either. It's over at the Dick Museum in Kilmarnock.'

'So when was this crannog made then?' John asked.

'I think it was back in the Roman times. They found some Roman pottery in there anyhow. I hae got a wee bit back at my hoose.' Jack then looked rather guiltily at John. 'It's just a wee bit that I found on the soil after they had left. It was too small for them to be interested.'

The rain started again, so John started to shut the gate. 'Well, that's an interesting history. Perhaps I will call in at the Dick Museum some time. In the meantime, let's get back to the steading, afore we need a boat oorselves.'

CHAPTER 3
1905

❧

M argaret Corbett Scott had packed up all that was precious to her, including a wedding dress, and took a ship from Scotland to Canada to be married to Hugh Baird. After safely taking horses and cattle from his native Ayrshire to the middle of the Canadian prairies, Hugh had constructed a home on the land that he had purchased and called the farm Mansfield, after the estate on which he was born. It wasn't a grand house, but it would be comfortable and would keep them warm during the cold winters that descended on McCauley in Manitoba. He would build something bigger and grander as time and money allowed.

A typical Canadian prairie farmhouse around 1900.

Margaret accepted the hospitality of some neighbours until her wedding day and quickly became part of the Scottish community that had grown in the area. Hugh and Margaret were married on 28 December in the house of a neighbour and the celebrations seemed to last beyond Hogmanay.

The McCauley community grew up around the railway line, which was their only real link with the rest of Canada. Until the community and the farms had developed sufficiently to provide most of their food, building materials and home comforts, everything had to come into McCauley by train. The freezing winters brought the opportunity for the Scottish immigrants to brush the snow off the frozen lakes and do some curling. Hugh had been a keen player back at home and frequently travelled to Loch o' the Lowes, just outside New Cumnock for practice and matches. In Scotland they played with curling stones shaped from granite. In McCauley they carved blocks of hard wood or sawn railway sleepers and attached handles made from whatever metal they could scrounge. With a wee dram afterwards, they could almost believe that they had recreated Scotland. However, a look up from the ice and the absence of any hills would quickly dispel that notion.

The Clydesdale horses that he brought over were much admired, but Hugh was more interested in their performance pulling a plough than in a show ring. To this end they did their job well and soon Hugh was growing fine crops of wheat, some of which could well end up in markets in the West of Scotland. His Ayrshire cattle were also providing the local families with milk and cheese, as well as plenty of healthy calves to grow the herd. Hugh was able to sell the bull calves at a good price, as the Garclaugh pedigree was now becoming famous amongst dairy farmers throughout the world. Garclaugh Spottie, which had been exported to America several years previously, had held the world record for the most milk produced in a year. Hugh made sure that all prospective buyers knew that his cattle came from the same herd and shared a heritage with this famous cow. He considered plans to travel back to Ayrshire in the following year in order to bring more horses and cattle over to McCauley.

***

At Meikle Garclaugh, Hugh's brother Andrew was busy selecting bulls and cows from his herd in order to produce another champion cow. Andrew was expecting a visit from Adam Montgomerie who was a local exporter, who arranged for cattle to be shipped across to the USA and Canada. Andrew had cleaned up a couple of his cows so that they would look their best for his inspection. In order that their horns would grow evenly and upwards he had constructed a pulley system in their box. A length of cord would be attached to the end of each horn. The cords would go upwards and through a couple of pulleys to steel weights that hung on each side of the pen. In this way the horn was being pulled upwards, but the cow could still move its head and feed or drink. Adam was leaning over the lower door looking at the apparatus that Andrew was explaining.

'At first glance it looks like some instrument of torture, Andrew,' he chuckled. 'The length that you breeders go to make sure that you win rosettes.'

'You would not be here wanting to buy my kye if it did'nae work,' Andrew retorted. 'Any advantage that I can gain will bring me higher prices.'

'They have to produce milk as well as look pretty,' Adam responded.

'And they do. I hope to produce another world champion soon. Lady Diana is due to calve soon from Herd Laddie. I have high hopes that it will be a guid yen,' Andrew said proudly.

'Which brings me to the subject of my visit. I have had a request from an American buyer for a couple of guid kye. Is this yen that you are torturing a guid yen?' Adam enquired.

'Aye, this yen is available, for the right price, of course. I have another twa that might suit yer needs. I'll take ye around to them now.' Andrew led Adam around to some more pens behind the byre. Adam inspected them, running his hand over their udders and noting the size of their milk vein that ran along their bellies. After a while he stood back and had one last look at them from further away. He removed his cap and brushed his hand over the thinning hair towards his brow.

'Right. Thank ye for that, Andrew. I have some more to see at Castle-mains Farm, but I may put in an offer for these two. What are their names?

'This yen is Garclaugh Bloomer and this yen is White Rose. The yen in the box is Brown Lady,' Andrew explained.

Adam wrote the names in his note book, followed by some more comments. He closed the book and pushed it back into his coat pocket.

'Thank ye, Andrew. I will most likely call around tomorrow to discuss prices.' Adam then strode purposely around to the yard to where his horse and gig were tethered. He climbed up onto the seat, gave Andrew a wave then rode up the track that led to the road to Mansfield and to Castlemains Farm, where the Sloan family farmed. Andrew rubbed his hands together and walked with a smile towards the house. He was making good money from the herd, his father would have been proud of his accomplishments.

Two weeks later Lady Diana calved and produced a heifer that Andrew named May Mischief. It looked a fine calf and Andrew was pleased. As he watched this calf tottering around on the straw trying to find its mother's teat, he did not know just how pleased he would be with this new addition to the Garclaugh herd.

CHAPTER 4
1906

ᕙᕗ

The wet weather of previous year had been followed by yet another damp summer and a winter of deep snow. The preceding year had also brought the family sadness, as well as poor weather, with news of Annie Stevenson's death. John had travelled down to visit Barbara as much as possible, to give her support, as well as satisfying his own desire to be by her side. The passing of Barbara's mother made Barbara realise that her life was changing and she wanted to control that change by getting married to John and starting their life together. John was also itching to find his own farm, so he told the Hay sisters that he would be seeking a farm tenancy somewhere. They were happy to support his ambition to move on and even offered to lend him money to get started. So it was that on a cold January morning John loaded his newly acquired bicycle onto the milk cart, along with the churns. Once he had sent his churns on their way to Glasgow, Jack took the cart back to the farm and John waited for a train that would take him and his bicycle to Carlisle.

John had been searching the adverts for available farm tenancies in the regional newspapers and had replied to a number of these advertisements. In the end he received replies from two farms, one in Kilmarnock and one in Cumberland. He preferred the description of the farm in Cumberland so he sent a telegram to the owner, asking if they could meet the next day. So it was that John was now on the train to Carlisle Station, from where he cycled the twenty-two miles to Silloth, close to the waters of the Solway Firth, to meet with Mr Kerr.

The land around Carlisle was similar to Ayrshire, with lots of undulating hills, small fields and with the hills of the Lake District just visible to the south. However, as he approached Wigton John found that the land was flatter and it was certainly easier to pedal his bicycle. As he approached the coastline, where Balladoyle was situated, there was hardly a rise in the ground to be seen anywhere. As he passed field gateways he could see flat fields stretching for many miles and few trees. The fields were also much more regular, where they had been measured out in rectangles following the draining of the marshland a hundred or so years previously.

John Kerr was both surprised and impressed to see this young man turn up at the farm on a bicycle, having cycled all the way from Carlisle, down some rough unmade roads.

'That's some journey that ye hae made. I was waiting to see a horse and gig arrive, not a bicycle,' John Kerr greeted John Baird.

'I was told it would be downhill from Carlisle, so I thought that a bicycle would do for the job,' John replied with a grin.

Mr Kerr gave a hearty laugh. 'Aye, but it will be uphill on the way back to Carlisle!' he responded, putting his hand on John's shoulder. It was clear that John Kerr had already taken a shine to the young fellow Scot.

'I own a couple of farms in this area, but I live at Redhall, the other side of Wigton. My nephew was farming Balladoyle, but he passed away last year, so the tenancy has come available,' Mr Kerr explained. 'There are one hundred and fifty acres in total at Balladoyle here. I assume that ye wid want to take on the whole farm?'

'Aye. I wid like to take it all on. The only problem wid be that I don't have a lot of money to buy stock and equipment. Wid ye see yer way to give me six months afore I have to pay rent?' John asked hopefully.

'Ye get yerself sorted on the farm and pay the rent when ye can.'

'That's very generous, Mr Kerr. I expected ye to ask me lots of questions afore ye consider me for the tenancy.'

'The reputation of the Bairds at Garclaugh precede ye, John. If ye have half of yer faither's acumen for farming, then ye will do well on this farm. Have ye got any questions for me, afore ye agree?

'What is likely to be the biggest problem that I will face on the farm?' John asked.

'Well, ye will have seen how the land is so low lying. Ye will have to work hard to keep the ditches clear, as the water takes a lang time to drain away. When we had that wet summer two years ago the water lay on the fields for most of the year. Will ye plan to bring some of the Garclaugh cattle doon here?'

'Aye. I will have to speak to my brother Andrew and see if he will gie us a guid price.'

John Kerr gave another hearty laugh. 'No discounts from yer brother then! But if ye need any horses, I have some guid Clydesdales that I can let ye have.'

The two men shook hands and John was invited for lunch by Mr Kerr at a hotel in Silloth, overlooking the seafront. Like many farmers in Cumberland, John Kerr was born over the border in Scotland. They talked about cows, horses and the price of milk. John came away with lots of useful advice about the area and recommendations for good tradesmen. The two men bade their farewells and John got back on his bicycle to cycle to Carlisle Station and return to Mid-Buiston Farm for the afternoon milking. Not only had he got his first step on the farming ladder, but he now had a farmhouse to bring a wife. He would get the farm and house sorted and then get married.

Unfortunately, John and Barbara's marriage plans were disrupted by yet more sad news for the Stevenson family. Just eighteen months after Barbara's mother passed away, her father, James, died after a short illness. It was the family's belief that his spirit left him at the same time as his wife Annie, so when he became ill, he seemed to have lost any will to get well again. During the hot summer, with record temperatures, Barbara stayed at Nether Cairn and mourned the loss of her father. Allan, Barbara's brother, inherited the tenancy and had married in the previous December. His wife Wilhemina was keen to get the house sorted to her liking and Barbara felt that the house was no longer her home. She was glad when John broached the subject of their marriage, but it would be many months before he felt that the farmhouse at Balladoyle would be good enough for them to set up home together.

While John was working on his new farm at Balladoyle in Cumberland, Hugh had travelled from Canada to collect some more horses and cattle for his farm. He stayed at Meikle Garclaugh with his mother and his brothers, Andrew, Gilbert and William and his sisters, Mary and Chrissie. During his stay he described the new life that he had made for himself and his plans for the future. At twenty years old, Gilbert was only slightly younger than Hugh when Hugh had made his first journey to Canada. Gilbert, like many younger sons, appreciated that he would have to forge his own way in the world, as there would not be a farm tenancy to inherit. He was enthralled by Hugh's stories of Canada and one day he approached Hugh with a question.

'Wid ye take me over with ye when to go back?'

Hugh paused before answering. 'I wid be happy to take ye with me. I wondered how lang it be wid afore ye asked,' Hugh replied. 'What wid ye plan to do over there?'

'Wid you take me on as a labourer on the farm, whilst I see what is aboot for me?' Gilbert asked.

Hugh step forward and put his hand on Gilbert's shoulder. 'I could not pay ye much. But ye wid get a bed and vittles.'

'That'll do fine,' Gilbert responded with a smile.

So it was that Hugh, Gilbert and a collection of Clydesdale horses and Ayrshire cattle took the ship *Lake Erie* from Liverpool to Montreal during the summer of 1906, bound for McCauley in the Canadian prairies.

***

Barbara endured a sweltering November, when temperatures were over thirty degrees, before her wedding date was eventually fixed for the first of June of the following year, 1907. She visited Balladoyle a number of times during that year to see how the house and the farm were progressing. She also exchanged letters with her brother David, who was making good progress himself within the world of high finance in London. David had moved on from being a bank clerk and was now working as a stockbroker's manager in the London Stock Exchange. David Stevenson had been describing life in London in his letters and Barbara was particularly interested to read of the exploits of the women suffragettes, who had recently stormed parliament in protest at the lack of progress in giving women the vote. This was a topic for which Barbara had a real passion; although her fiancé John Baird did not have any strong opinions on the subject, he had learned not to raise the topic in conversation.

The spring of 1907 was taking its time to shake off the cold air of winter. So, the guests arriving at Nether Cairn had to wear coats to John and Barbara's wedding, even though it was June. All of the Baird and

Stevenson family had travelled, except for Hugh and Gilbert who were still a few thousand miles away. David Stevenson had travelled back to his childhood home from Southend-on-Sea, where he had recently bought a new three-bedroomed house in the suburbs, a house that befitted a member of the London Stock Exchange.

Allan Stevenson's wife, Wilhemina, was in charge of the refreshments, even though she was nursing their newly born son, James. John's brother, Thomas, had come over from Birnieknowe with his wife Elizabeth and their two children. Barbara would have liked her sister Jessie to have come over from Castlemains Farm to help her get ready for the wedding, but since having married Mungo Sloan just five years previously she had produced two sons and a daughter. She was still nursing her daughter Annie, so it was difficult for her to come over earlier, however, they had promised to try and make it over for the ceremony.

The Church of Scotland minister arrived towards noon to officiate at the ceremony, which would take place in the living room, where Jessie had got married. James, Barbara's eldest brother, would give her away at the service. As Barbara stood outside in the corridor with her brother, she felt the absence of her father and mother. She wiped away some tears from her eyes and her brother misinterpreted the reason for her apparent sadness and made a remark about not worrying about the wedding. She turned to look at him and made herself smile. She had been yearning for this wedding for too long and she would make it the happiest day of her life. As she walked into the room John turned to look at her. She gasped in delight at the sight of this handsome man, whom she adored, standing waiting for her. She hardly heard all the words that the minister was saying and then all of sudden she was being asked if she would take this man to be her husband. She almost said 'Yes, please' too early. Then she heard the words 'I pronounce you man and wife' and everyone in the room was congratulating her. At last she would be able to start her new life as Barbara Baird at Balladoyle Farm in Cumberland.

CHAPTER 5
1910

_◎◁◊▷◎_

Gilbert had returned from his visit to Hugh's Canadian farm full of stories for the family. It was clear that he was keen to emulate his brother's venture. His mother, however, had dampened his enthusiasm, telling him, in no uncertain terms, that he had responsibilities on the farm, particularly as his brother Andrew's health was getting worse.

Chrissie was now working full time as a dairymaid and learning how to make cheese and cream from the milk that the cows were providing. It had now been accepted that drinking milk from cows that had bovine tuberculosis was responsible for the human tuberculosis that ravaged so many people, particularly the young. The Glenafton Sanatorium that had been built on the hillside above New Cumnock was largely filled with tuberculosis sufferers. Fortunately, a vaccination against tuberculosis had been developed, although it had not yet been made widely available. In the meantime, regulations had been introduced to ensure that milk was clean and dairy farms were inspected regularly and given a certificate of cleanliness. Dairy farmers could then use this certificate to advertise their milk and get a better price.

The cows and bulls of the Garclaugh herd continued to win prizes at shows across Scotland, and Andrew had recently achieved awards for both the best cow and the best bull in the New Cumnock Annual Show. He had not entered his best cow, called May Mischief, into the show as he had even greater ambitions for this young cow. He had contacted the various local cattle exporters, who worked with American breeders, to let them know that he had another potential champion Ayrshire cow. He wanted a high price for this cow and he would hold out until he got it.

Garclaugh cows formed the bulk of the Ayrshire herd that John had put together at Balladoyle. They had already started to produce young ones, as had Barbara, giving birth to a bonnie boy a year after their marriage. In the Scottish tradition he was named John after his paternal grandfather. Barbara had settled into life in Cumberland and enjoyed walks to Silloth, which was now quite a tourist town. Wee John was now toddling about the house and Barbara was finding it hard to catch up with him. The farm was paying its way, so they could afford a couple of maids to help with the house work and cook for a growing work force. John had three young labourers working for him, all of whom lived on the farm.

As John Kerr, the landlord, had indicated previously, the land the made up Balladoyle was low-lying and slow draining. John had spent much of his first year at the farm cleaning the ditches, so that rain water would drain away as quickly as possible. He also limed the fields to encourage better grass and crops of corn. He also decided to invest in some good Clydesdale horses that he could use for breeding. Mr Kerr had several champion Clydesdale horses and was happy to sell John a two-year-old filly that was registered in the Clydesdale Stud Book. John was pleased that he had a good pedigree horse, however, its main task was not impressing judges in a parade ring, but would be pulling a plough.

Barbara was visiting a neighbouring farm, to speak with Catherine Wright. Catherine had been recently widowed and was trying to keep her farm going on her own. She had a good farm manager, but was struggling to make enough money to cover costs. Barbara had met her soon after she moved in and appreciated her no-nonsense manner. Barbara had brought wee John, who was playing in the garden in the late May sunshine.

'I'm so pleased you came to visit, Barbara,' Catherine confessed. 'I needed to take a break from dairy work. My hands feel like two bannocks they are so dry. Now how's the bairn progressing?'

'We are all fine, thank ye for asking, Catherine. As ye see, wee John is full of energy and growing fast. John dotes on his wee son, it's amusing watching how John smiles when he sees his wee son.'

'I have seen you walking past on yer way to Silloth. You clearly enjoy visiting the town,' Catherine remarked.

'Aye, well John is so busy on the farm, it's nice to get away and see all the visitors on the sea front. I grew up on a remote farm and all my visits to the local town were supervised by my parents. It's nice just to wander on my own with the bairn,' Barbara mused.

'Did you read the dreadful news from Whitehaven? Such a tragedy.'

'No. What news is that?' Barbara asked.

'There has been an explosion at the Wellington Pit. The pit has caught fire and they can't get the men out. They sent in a rescue team, but the rescue team didn't return. They think that they too have been overcome by the fumes from the fire,' Catherine explained.

'Oh, that's dreadful. How many men do they think are doon the pit?' Barbara asked.

'Over a hundred, they think. The wives, mothers and children are waiting at the pithead for news, but it's likely to be bad news for so many of them.'

'What with the death of the king, we've had some bad news in the last couple of weeks,' Barbara commented.

'Aye. Let's hope that the new King George's reign brings prosperity and peace. I wonder when his coronation will take place? Presumably it will be next summer. That'll be a chance for some dancing Barbara.' Catherine laughed, before abruptly stopping as she thought of the many widows who would not be celebrating at Whitehaven.

***

News of the death of King Edward VII quickly reached the prairie towns of Canada. Firstly, by the amazing new Marconi radio transmissions, that allowed voice messages to be sent from Britain to Newfoundland, and then on by telegraph. The news was of interest to many of the residents of McCauley, but not to the many immigrants who had come over from regions of Europe that had suffered from the wars between neighbouring kings. They were happy to get away from the famines and persecution that dominated their previous existences and they now worked hard to create a peaceful and successful life for their children. The barren prairie that Hugh had viewed from the train window, when he travelled west from Montreal, was now becoming covered with golden fields of wheat and herds of farm animals.

Hugh, Maggie and their young son Jack had travelled over to Ayrshire two years previously, to collect more horses and Ayrshire cattle for his farm. Some of the animals he sold to neighbouring farmers, but the best ones he kept for breeding with his existing herd. His horses and cattle were greatly admired locally and won prizes on the local agricultural fairs. But as autumn approached Hugh and Maggie would be looking forward to the birth of their second child. Hugh was already building an extension to the small cottage to accommodate his growing family.

Gilbert had written to Hugh and told him that he still wished to come over and start a new life in Canada. As soon as Andrew's health improved, he intended to take a ship to Montreal. Hugh pondered on the letter. He wondered if Andrew's health would improve sufficiently and that Gilbert would find himself being persuaded to stay on at Meikle Garclaugh.

***

At Meikle Garclaugh Andrew was fit enough to welcome a visit by an American farmer, who was interested in buying May Mischief, his prize young cow. Andrew had welcomed a number of prospective buyers over the previous months, who had all been very impressed with May Mischief. However, none of them were prepared to pay the high price that Andrew demanded. A gig containing two men arrived in the yard at Garclaugh and Andrew walked across to greet them.

'Good morning, Mr Baird,' said the older of the two men held his hand out to Andrew.

'Good morning, Adam,' Andrew replied and then turned to the second gentleman.

'This is Mr Percival Roberts from the United States,' Adam Montgomerie announced. Adam Montgomerie was the cattle exporter based at Ochiltree, not far from New Cumnock. He had exported a number of Andrew's cattle over the years.

'I'm pleased to meet you, Mr Baird. I am a great admirer of your cows and have Garclaugh Bloomer in the Penhurst herd. I have also got White Beauty and plan to breed some fine stock from them both,' Percival Roberts bragged.

'I'm pleased to meet you as well, Mr Roberts, and I am also pleased that Bloomer is doing well. Would you like to come in for some tea or coffee?' Andrew invited.

The three men entered the house at Garclaugh where they were introduced to Flora. They talked cows for quite a while before they then left
to visit the pens to look at the cows and bulls that Andrew was hoping
to sell. Percy Roberts showed an interest in all the cattle that he was
shown, but in particular May Mischief, however, he did not want to
show his hand before the negotiations started over a purchase, so did
not give May Mischief special attention. He could see that May
Mischief was a special cow and he decided there and then that he
wanted her, whatever the price. The negotiations did not last long as
Andrew refused to move from the price that he had placed on May
Mischief. Percy Roberts could see that Andrew was immovable, so
agreed to pay the high price. So it was that another one of the
Garclaugh herd travelled across the Atlantic to new pastures, while
Andrew Baird travelled across to his bank to deposit a large cheque.

***

Farming prospered as the British Empire created more markets for
industrial products and agricultural produce. Europe was at peace,
which allowed trade to expand across the globe. Hugh in Canada was
able to get a good price for the wheat that he harvested and which was
shipped to Britain, just as Andrew was able to get good prices for the
cattle that he shipped across the Atlantic. Tom at Birnieknowe Farm
was also breeding Ayrshires from Garclaugh cows and bulls and was
hoping to match his brother's success. The youngest brother Gilbert
had not yet found his route to success, so he carried on working and
learning at Garclaugh, while he dreamt of working on pastures closer to
his brother Hugh in Canada. Their father would be proud of the
progress that his sons were making in the farming world, as well as his
two daughters who showed their skills in the dairy.

CHAPTER 6

1912

⌾⌇⌒⌇⌾

In the previous year at Balladoyle, John and Barbara had produced a second son, who they named James, after Barbara's father. John was very proud of his two sons and he was devoted to his Barbara. Like his sons the farm was growing well under John's stewardship. He had improved the soil in the fields through much hard work, cleaning out old ditches and creating new ones. He had spread slag and minerals to improve the soil for grass and the cows that grazed on the rich pastures became healthy and produced plenty of milk. John had been investigating ways to sell his milk for a higher price and had found a dairy in Newcastle that would take his milk, but wanted more than his herd could produce. John had approached neighbouring farms to see if he could set up a cooperative to provide the milk that the Newcastle dairy required.

The beach at Silloth

Silloth had grown as a tourist and leisure resort, but it also had a port that served the local area and allowed ships to bring raw materials to nearby factories. A railway line had been built from the port to Carlisle and beyond. This railway line provided John the opportunity to transport milk to the cities and John was keen to grab that opportunity. So, along with a partner, they were negotiating an agreement with a processing dairy in Newcastle, so that they and other farmers in a cooperative could rely on a regular income for their milk.

As well as finding ways to make more money from his dairy herd, John was also breeding pedigree horses that he could sell locally and further afield. Every farm needed horse-power to be able to move carts, plough fields and transport produce to customers. Mr Kerr, his landlord, gave John regular advice about breeding Clydesdales and was generally very happy about the way that John was running Balladoyle.

A neighbouring farm owned by John Kerr had also become available, after the farmer became too poorly to carry on and the tenancy that had become vacant. John was offered this farm as well and he didn't need to be asked twice. Pelutho Mire bordered onto Balladoyle so John knew about the soil and how to improve it. It would give John the opportunity to expand the herd onto a larger acreage of grass and grow more cereal crops.

After a hot summer the previous year John was hoping for another good summer. However, the rain had arrived in the spring and it did not look as if it was going to move on very soon. John opened the back door of the back place and shook the rain off his coat.

'This rain!' John shouted through to the kitchen where Barbara was feeding baby James. 'I put the kye on the meadows when it looked as if they were drying up, and now the beast are up to their bellies in mud. I'll have to try and find some stones to put in the gateways so that we can get in and oot more easily.'

There was no reply from the kitchen. John removed his muddy boots and went through to the warmth of the kitchen.

'Did ye say something, John?' Barbara asked.

'No. I was just bleating aboot the rain. Not that it will do any guid,' John replied in a resigned tone.

Baby James was staring wide eyed at his father, who started making strange faces at him. James burst out crying.

'Now look what you've done. It will take an age to get him quiet again,' Barbara complained as she lifted James out of the high chair. 'There's the postie, go and collect the letters.'

There was a loud knock on the front door as John made his way along the corridor. The cheery face of Percy Brown, the postman, was holding out a number of letters as John opened the door.

'Good morning, Mr Baird. I hope all is well with you and your family,' Percy greeted John.

'Aye. We're all well here. It wid be better if this rain wid stop though,' John replied.

'But it's the rain the makes your grass green and yer cows fat, Mr Baird,' Percy responded with a laugh and a wave, as he climbed back onto his bicycle.

John closed the front door and looked through the letters.

'There's one for you from London,' John told Barbara. 'I'll leave it on the table for you.'

John then took the other business letters through to the parlour where he had installed a desk. He opened the various bills and correspondence. One letter was from the dairy in Newcastle describing the conditions that they wanted to apply to the contract with the cooperative of dairy farmers that John was establishing around Silloth. He wanted to share the good news with Barbara, so he made his way back to the kitchen. Barbara was standing engrossed in the letter from London that she had opened.

'What's the letter? It looks serious,' John asked.

'It's from Jane. David's not at all well and has been poorly for a few weeks. She's worried that he may not recover,' Barbara recounted, as she looked up from the letter. 'Poor David and poor Jane, having to look after him with no family nearby. She must be feeling so lonely. I wonder if I could go down to stay with them for a while, John.'

Jane was the wife of Barbara's brother David, who worked in the City of London as a stockbroker. They both lived in a salubrious suburb of London in a large three-bedroom semi-detached house in Southend, but a long distance from their roots. Barbara knew Jane from before she married her brother, so they had written letters to each other for some years. Barbara could feel Jane's distress in the words of the letter and yearned to go down to London to support her.

'Barbara, do you ken how far it is to Southend, let alone London? It is a lang journey for anyone to take, but doubly so for someone who is pregnant,' John pointed out.

'Och, I'm only a few weeks pregnant. It's no like I am ill,' Barbara responded.

'And what would happen to the bairn?' John asked.

'I could take wee James with me. It would be guid for Jane and John to see the wee yen. Wee John wid be alright to stay here. Mary, the maid, is very guid with him and she can manage.' Barbara seemed to have decided.

'I can see that ye have made yer mind up.' John sighed. 'When were yer planning to set off?'

'As soon as I can. Perhaps George can take me in the gig over to the station in Silloth and get the tickets that I will need? I can also send a telegram to Jane and get her to give directions to their house from Southend station. It'll be quite an adventure,' she confessed.

John pondered Barbara's plans and his anxiety about the long journey showed on his face.

'Don't make a fuss, John, I'll be fine. I will stay a week or two, then I will head back. Perhaps I can take wee James to the beach? Jane says that it is a short trip away, not that she will want to leave David. I do hope that he will make a recovery and that he has not picked up tuberculosis,' Barbara worried.

'They have this new vaccine now for TB,' John responded.

'Aye, but you have to take that before you are exposed to infected milk. That's why they are giving it to the wains first,' Barbara explained.

Both Barbara and John had witnessed the dreadful progression of tuberculosis in both children and adults. It was not something that they wanted to witness with any of their loved ones. John always kept a close watch on his cattle and removed any animals that showed evidence of TB themselves. He wanted to get his herd tested for TB, as he had heard that there was now a reliable test available. Unfortunately, the test was not yet widely available and was expensive.

The next day Barbara set off for the station at Silloth with George, one of their workers, driving the gig. Silloth had been very busy over the Easter weekend and she had managed to persuade John to get away from his cows and horses and visit the seafront with the boys. Easter had been in early April that year, but fortunately the rain had paused to allow the visitors to enjoy themselves beneath some sunshine. She visited the station and sorted out the tickets for the long train journey. It would involve the short trip to Carlisle and then a long trip down with the Midlands Railway to Euston Station. From Euston she would be able to take a local train to Southend, where she could pick up a taxi for David and Jane's house. As she left the station, she saw a group of people crowded around a newspaper vendor. She could see by the reactions of the people reading the newspaper that there must be some bad news. As she approached the gig, she could see that George was also engrossed in a newspaper.

'What's the news, George?' she asked as George came around the gig to help her climb in.

'There's been a dreadful ship sinking, with hundreds drowned. It is the Titanic, that huge ship that they built at Belfast that they reckoned was unsinkable. Well, it's sunk,' George responded bluntly.

Barbara took the newspaper, which showed the headline 'Titanic Sinks, 1500 Die'.

'Oh, dear God!' she exclaimed. 'Fifteen-hundred deaths. That is just dreadful. How could a ship like that sink with so many lives lost? Only six-hundred and seventy-five saved,' she asked no-one in particular.

'I expect that they got the wealthy ones off first though,' George commented.

Barbara did not reply to George's comment as she studied the newspaper to absorb more details of the tragedy. They shared snippets of the news story, bewildered by the enormity of it all. When she got back to Balladoyle, she sat for quite a while in the kitchen until Mary, the maid, came through with wee John, who was crying for his mother, and Barbara was back into her role in charge of the household.

***

The news of the sinking of the Titanic reached the prairies of Canada very quickly as telegraph messages were sent down the lines that bordered the railway. Newspapers travelled with passengers, so even in a small town like McAuley the residents were digesting the news. Hugh was busy on the farm when Maggie came back from the shops with the newspapers. The winter frosts had now eased and Hugh was keen to get the spring corn in the ground. Winters are harsh on the prairies, with the temperature rarely getting above freezing between November and March. In some years the snow lay many feet thick on the ground and the bitter north wind can blow it into drifts that would bury a cottage. All newcomers would quickly learn to put in a good quantity of wood in the store to get them through those five winter months.

There was still a cold wind, despite the thaw, so Hugh made his way over to the cottage for a hot cup of coffee.

'There's more news of this sinking of the Titanic that we heard aboot yesterday. There are a lot of folks drowned,' Maggie told Hugh, when he had found a chair in the kitchen. As he read the story his son Alex tottered towards him and took hold of his leg. Hugh looked away from the newspaper.

'Hello, wee man. How are you this morning?' Hugh asked Alex.

'Gee gee, dada,' Alex replied.

'Oh, you want to see the gee-gees do ye? Well, I'm sure that we can sort ye oot.'

'It's still cold ootside, Hugh. You'll need to get him wrapped up. Wee

John has already been ootside this morning and he didn't last lang afore he was complaining of cold fingers,' Maggie pointed out.

'Aye I'll get him wrapped up and he can come with me oot to the stables.'

'Oh, there's a letter from Gilbert,' Maggie remembered, handing Hugh the letter that she had collected from the post office.

Hugh opened it and read through the letter that Gilbert had written. After a while he put the letter down on the table.

'Well? What news from hame?' Maggie asked, impatient for the news.

'Aye well. They all seem well, although Andrew is no better. Ma's well, as are Mary and Chrissie. William is still healthy. Tom and Elizabeth have had another girl and he has made good progress improving Birnieknowe. I don't understand why he stays up on that hill. It is so bleak up there.' Maggie gave him an impatient look, as he was not telling her the news she wanted to hear.

'John seems to be getting on very well down in Cumberland. Their wee James is doing well, as is wee John. Gilbert has been doon to visit them and help oot. He says the land around Balladoyle is very low-lying and that John seems to spend half his time digging ditches. Gilbert says that he has taken on another neighbouring farm as well. Aye well, John's always been a worker. His landlord is a top Clydesdale breeder, so John has bought a mare in foal and is hoping to do some breeding of his own. But, the main point of his letter is that he is still keen to come oot here and has told ma and Andrew that he intends to leave Garclaugh.' Hugh finished his summary of Gilbert's letter and handed it over to Maggie.

'You were talking aboot going back over next year to get some more stock. Perhaps he could come back with us?' Maggie speculated.

'Aye. Perhaps.' Hugh was non-committal. 'As long as he doesn't expect me to nursemaid him. The farm won't easily keep another mouth to feed over the winter.'

'Och, I'm sure Gilbert realises that. He is yer brother, Hugh. Give him a chance to make his ain way over here,' Maggie responded.

'Aye. Yer right.' Gilbert leaned forward and picked up his son. 'Now then, wee Alex, let's get ye dressed up to help me and wee John with the horses.'

Hugh and his sons were soon out in the cold wind getting the horses brushed down and harnessed up ready for a cart. John and Alex had grown up around the farm animals but Hugh was conscious that the farm was a dangerous place. The large hooves of the Clydesdales could easily crush a young boy's foot. Hugh lifted Alex onto the horse's back, but it wasn't long before John was also wanting to join his brother.

'Now you hold tight to the harness whilst we go into this field.'

Maggie watched the three of them through the window of the cottage, before going back to preparing supper. She was content with her new life, despite being far from her family. The McAuley community were supportive and friendly; they were like a replacement family. During the winter months there were many community events when they could all get together and share news, while the freeze stopped most outdoor work.

***

Barbara had packed a suitcase with everything that she and James would need for the trip down to Southend-on-Sea. John had taken her and the boys along to the railway stop at Blackdyke, where he took the churns for the milk train. It was just a platform alongside the track. They would have to wave down the train as it came along the track from Silloth. The promise of better weather after Easter had proved to be false and it was cold and wet for early May. Fortunately, the rain had held off that morning.

'Now, you've got yer tickets for Carlisle?' John asked Barbara.

'Aye, John. You saw me put them all in my bag this morning,' Barbara responded, slightly impatiently. Barbara knew that John was still worried about her making the journey on her own. She was a little anxious herself, but was also excited about seeing her brother David. She had received a letter from Jane just two days previously, telling them that David's health was greatly improved, which removed some of the anxiety that Barbara was feeling. She also gave Barbara details of how to find their home in Westcliffe-on-Sea, a suburb of Southend.

The train appeared down the track, so John waved his arms to make sure that the driver had seen that there were passengers to board. Wee John got very excited about the arrival of the train, whereas James was looking much more uncertain. The screech of the brakes and the clouds of steam made James's face crumple into tears. Barbara picked him up as John trundled the suitcase down to the baggage car. She bent down to give wee John a cuddle.

'Now you be a good boy and help daddy. Mary will be looking after you, so you must do what she tells you.'

'I want to go on the train too,' wee John whined.

'But daddy needs you to help him. Will you do that?'

Wee John seemed unconvinced, but reached up to hold his father's hand when he came back along to platform.

'Now look after yerself, Barbara, and send me a telegram to let me know that you have arrived safely.' John gave his wife a hug and opened the door of the carriage so that she could climb in while holding baby James. The train was already starting to move towards Carlisle when John had barely closed to door. He lifted wee John and the two of them waved at the departing train.

'Right then, young man. Let's get back hame and make sure that everyone is doing what they are supposed to be doing,' John said to his young son.

Barbara's journey to Southend-on Sea was long but uneventful. There were porters on hand at each station to help her with the heavy suitcase and a very helpful guard allowed her to use his van for sorting out James, as it was more comfortable than a usual brake van. Her fellow passengers in their compartment were friendly, but Barbara could tell that they most like had had very little experience of babies and their nappies, so she was glad to be able to use the table in the guard's van. The train that she boarded at Carlisle travelled all the way to Euston Station in north London, so she was able to stay in her compartment and even managed to get a little sleep when wee James allowed it. James was active, but she managed to keep him entertained and reasonably happy on the long journey.

They reached London by the middle of the afternoon. The station was the usual bustle of passengers and porters that would typify any of the London stations. Barbara found a porter to collect her suitcase and move it to the platform from where she would be able to take the train to Southend-on-Sea. When they reached the end of the platform, they entered the great hall. The huge classical hall, with stone pillars, had a ceiling that was over sixty feet high. Barbara gazed upwards and gasped, it looked like a cathedral. James pointed to a large statue of some eminent looking man on a plinth at the base of a grand staircase.

'That's Robert Stephenson, young man,' the porter told him. 'He designed these railways.' He then turned to Barbara, as it was clear that she had never seen Euston Station before. 'If you look up at the top of the walls you can see stone pictures of the various cities that are visited by the London and North Western Railway. That one over there is supposed to be Birmingham, but I can't see why.' Barbara studied the panel to which the porter pointed.

'It's the Southend-on-Sea that you are trying to reach? I think that you will need to get a train from platform four, but if you wait here, then I will check with the booking office.'

Barbara sat down on one of the benches that were placed inside the great hall. This gave her time to take in the immense surroundings. The roof was a criss-cross of stone beams. She wondered how they managed to stay up without falling, the ceiling looked so heavy. James was still looking at the large statue of Robert Stephenson.

'That man has a name that sounds like my family's, James,' Barbara told the uninterested toddler.

Euston Station main hall c1910.

The porter returned with information about the platform where the correct train would be found and helped Barbara with the suitcase. They were soon settled in a carriage and the train set off, taking them below and over bridges through the outskirts of London. They eventually arrived at Southend-on-Sea Station. James was now very fractious and clearly tired from the long journey. Barbara was having difficulty carrying him as he was twisting in her arms. Outside the station she looked around for a gig to take them to David and Jane's house. A porter waved to a waiting taxi, which moved forward in front of them. The suitcase was loaded, the porter given a tip and they were soon on their way through the town. Southend had expanded greatly with the arrival of the railways and was now a popular commuter town for London. There were many parallel streets of three-bedroomed semi-detached houses that had been constructed for the growing middle classes, to which Barbara's brother now belonged. The gig eventually arrived at Westcliffe-on-Sea and David and Jane's house as the daylight was starting to fade. It had been a long day travelling from Silloth, but it was a journey that would have taken two or three days just sixty years previously.

Barbara saw the door of the house open and Jane rushing down the garden path to greet her and James. The driver unloaded the suitcase and carried it to the door of the house. Jane welcomed Barbara into the house, where David was sitting in a chair in the parlour. Although he looked pale and thin, he was smiling and gave his sister as big a hug as he could manage from a sitting position. Barbara was so relieved to have reached her destination and sat with a sigh into the chair next to her brother. Wee James, who had been standing in the doorway staring at the strange surroundings, was not at all impressed at being ignored by his mother and proceeded to give a huge wail. Barbara's rest in the chair was short-lived.

***

At Garclaugh, Gilbert was busy brushing down one of the Clydesdale horses that he had been using to roll a field of grass, ready for the hay-making in the summer. They usually made hay on the river meadows, which often flooded in the winter and deposited a layer of silt and organic matter that acted as an excellent fertiliser. Since Tom, his brother, had left the farm Gilbert had taken charge of the horses. He had found himself as the head ploughman and had worked hard to develop his skills with the plough. He had also entered a couple of ploughing competitions, although had never quite managed to get the top prizes. He was keen to win some of these prizes, as he hoped that it would help him get one of the grants that the government were offering to skilled ploughmen to travel to empire countries, such as Canada. There was also a sense of pride that pushed him to achieve the high standards that he knew would have made his father proud.

Flora, his mother, pushed her sons hard to achieve their best and often reminded Gilbert about his father's high standards and work ethic. Gilbert was only fifteen when his father died following a heart attack. He always felt that he was overlooked when all the repercussions of his untimely death were being sorted. His elder brothers argued about the inheritance money and how it should be divided, while he was ignored. He had watched Tom and John get married, start families and farming careers, while Andrew steadily grew a reputation for breeding high-quality Ayrshire cows. Flora had persuaded Gilbert to stay on at Garclaugh to help Andrew, who suffered from pernicious anaemia, but now he wanted to move on. He had not yet received a reply to the letter that he had written to Hugh, who he hoped would help him get set up in Canada with his own farm.

Some light rain started to fall and Gilbert realised that he had been day-dreaming. He looked up at the grey clouds that threatened yet more rain.

'Come on then, beauty, let's get you back in the stables,' Gilbert told the horse that he had been brushing. 'I know how much you hate rain.'

***

Down in Essex Barbara had spent a relaxing three weeks with her brother David and his wife Jane. David was now on the road to recovery and had shaken off the illness that had looked so desperate the previous month. Barbara was conscious that the farm work back at Balladoyle would be growing and that she should be back to help out. She was also missing her elder son, wee John. Wee James had enjoyed his stay in Southend, despite his initial nervousness around his uncle and aunt. He loved running down the sand when they went for a trip to the beach and it clearly reminded him of home, when Barbara took her sons over to the Silloth beach.

Barbara was packing her suitcase in her room, ready for her journey home the next morning, when her brother David came into the room.

'It's been lovely having you to stay for the past weeks and seeing wee James. Jane and I have enjoyed having the wee yen around the house. I must admit that I had forgotten how nice it is to feel part of a family,' David confessed.

'You'll always be part of a family, David. You need to find some time to get away from the money making that has made you ill and visit us up north. Allan and Williamina's boys have filled the cairn with the sound of children again and Jessie and Mungo seem to be producing a bairn every year,' Barbara laughed. She put her hands on her abdomen. 'And I'm trying to keep up with her.'

David stepped forward to give his sister a hug.

'Aye, You're right. I'll see if we can find some time later on in the year to come up north and visit everyone. We have still to see yer home in Cumberland. Now, you have a safe journey home and look after that ambitious husband of yours. I can see him doing great things in the future.'

Barbara paused and then looked at her brother. She realised how much she was missing being at Balladoyle with the husband she adored.

'There's a wee boy I am greatly missing up at Balladoyle, so it will be good to get hame,' Barbara mused and returned to her packing.

Early the next morning the packed suitcase and wee James were loaded onto a gig for the trip to the station and the start of the long journey home. Barbara had made her farewells to David and Jane and now they were waiting at Euston Station to get the train to Birmingham. The station was a bustle of activity, as usual, and she was trying to find a porter to help get her suitcase onto the correct train. She glanced anxiously at the large clock in the great hall, which showed that the departure time was approaching. She needed to get James onto the train and settled, but could not leave the suitcase unattended. Eventually she got the attention of a porter and cajoled him into transporting her suitcase, rather than another traveller. The porter heaved the suitcase onto a trolley then walked briskly towards the platform with Barbara struggling to move wee James. He had spotted a dog that he wanted to stroke. In the end she lifted her son and rushed after the porter, who had almost disappeared from view.

She rushed along the platform bumping into other passengers. She saw that the porter was loading her suitcase into the baggage carriage, so she turned her attention to finding a suitable compartment in the train. The train was very full, as it was about to depart, but eventually she managed to find space in a carriage with three gentlemen, all of whom were smoking cigars. One of the men leered at her as she settled down on the bench seat and he whispered some comment to his neighbour, who then leered at Barbara as well and the two of them chuckled. Barbara felt very uncomfortable, but there was little chance of changing carriages until the train stopped at Birmingham.

At Birmingham Barbara had to change trains, so she was glad escape from the cigar smoke and salacious looks from the men who shared the compartment with her. James was getting fractious as they reached the platform, which was even more crowded than Euston. She had to barge her way towards the baggage carriage to make sure that her suitcase was being unloaded and would be put on to the correct train for Carlisle. She was getting hot and bothered. This was not a pleasant experience.

A damp mist had descended on Birmingham as her train pulled out of New Street Station with its vast iron and glass roof. The smoke from hundreds of chimneys that serviced the many industries in Birmingham had mixed with the mist and created an atmosphere as unpleasant as the cigar smoke that had filled the carriage from London. Barbara yearned for the clean air that blew down the Solway Firth and across the farmland at Balladoyle. She was tired and had strained her back carrying James to the carriage at Euston. She felt a twinge in the muscles of her abdomen. She winced and adjusted her position on the bench to make herself more comfortable. There was still a long journey ahead.

As the train approached Crewe for its next stop, Barbara felt another twinge in her abdomen. Barbara rubbed her lower stomach. It felt like contractions, but she was only four months pregnant, so that couldn't be the cause. Perhaps it was all this rich food that she had been eating while she was staying with her brother. James was asleep on her lap and she was sharing her compartment with an older couple who did not talk much and were happy to read books. Barbara was thankful for the quiet.

At Crewe the train took on more passengers and two gentlemen joined them in the compartment. The two men talked loudly about some business deal and so the quiet was broken. James also woke up and clearly needed his nappy changed. Barbara took him along to the small toilet cubicle to change him, but it was not designed for mothers and their needs. James shuffled about and Barbara struggled to get the dirty nappy off without making a mess. While Barbara was bending over, she felt another twinge in her abdomen and felt as if she needed to go to the toilet herself. She manoeuvred James towards the door and sat on the toilet, however, when she went to clean herself, she saw blood on the toilet tissue. It was not much, but its presence gave her a shiver of anxiety. This should not be happening. She sorted herself and James and returned to the compartment, with all sorts of worrying thoughts going through her mind. Was she losing the baby? Was this some other problem? There was not a lot that she could do sitting on a train. She would just have to wait until she reached home.

Unfortunately, Barbara's condition could not wait until she reached home. The contractions became more frequent and it was now clear to Barbara that she was having a miscarriage. She asked the couple to keep an eye on James while she went to the toilet again, only to find yet more blood. She used one of James' cotton nappies to try and absorb as much of it as she could, but she knew that it would only get worse. At Manchester, the couple left the train and the compartment emptied, which gave her the chance the lie down on the bench. James thought that this was a great game and did not give Barbara much rest. The train stopped at Lancaster and a young couple of Barbara's age entered the compartment. The wife could see that Barbara was not well and asked if she could help.

'Aye. Could you keep an eye on the bairn whilst I go to the toilet?' Barbara asked.

The lady was happy to do so, although James was not at all happy at her mother leaving him in the compartment and as Barbara made her way down the corridor, she could hear him started to cry. When Barbara reached the toilet, she could feel herself started to push. It was clear that she was losing the baby. Barbara lost sense of time and was startled by a banging on the door.

'Are you alright in there?' Barbara heard the woman's voice say.

'No. I'm not at all well. Can you look after the bairn until we get to Carlisle?' Barbara replied.

'I'll call the guard and see if he can find a doctor on the train,' the woman told Barbara.

'Thank you,' was all that Barbara could say.

There was no doctor on board, but when the train reached Carlisle Barbara was helped from the train and taken to the hotel next to the station. James was still crying and upset by the strange people who were taking him away from his mother. A doctor was called and a telegram was sent to Balladoyle.

John arrived as it was getting dark and rushed to Barbara's bedside.

'I've lost the bairn, John,' was all that Barbara could say.

John struggled to find some words of comfort. He kissed her gently on her forehead and held her hand.

The next day John took Barbara and James back home. Barbara had lost a lot of blood and was very weak. She was also mentally weak from the loss of her baby.

She tried get up and do some work around the house, but she started a fever so had to return to her bed. The fever became more intense over the next few days and the doctor was very concerned for Barbara. John watched as his wife drifted in and out of consciousness, desperate that there was nothing that he could do to help. Then on the 12 June Barbara passed away, her body unable to fight the infection brought on by the miscarriage. She was just thirty-five years old.

CHAPTER 7
1914

꩜

Hugh, Maggie and their three children had travelled over from Canada just before Christmas the previous year. Following the loss of the Titanic and over 1500 lives, passengers on the Canadian Pacific Railway Company ship *Lake Manitoba* had been understandably nervous when they spotted large icebergs from the deck, however, they had arrived safely in Liverpool. British international prestige had been dented by the loss of the 'unsinkable' Titanic, as had the news that Captain Scott had failed in his bid to lead the first expedition to the South Pole and his party had perished in the attempt.

Hugh and Maggie were staying at Meikle Garclaugh, so their children, John, Alex and Margaret were surrounded by Ayrshire cows and Clydesdale horses, just as they would have been back at their home in McAuley. The difference being that Scotland was not covered with deep snow. In fact, it had been a mild but wet start to the year with floods in many areas. The River Nith had breached its banks and the bottom meadows were flooded. It made the river look several times wider than usual.

Flora enjoyed having her grandchildren around, although she still dominated the house and gave formidable stares if any of the children failed to follow her rules. Mary and Chrissie were especially pleased to hear the laughter of the youngsters around the house. At one of the family meals the children were dismissed and went outside to play, while the adults remained around the dinner table.

'Have ye heard from John recently? How's he managing with the twa wains on his own?' Maggie asked Flora.

'Och, he's taken in a woman to run the house and look after the boys. Chrissie went doon soon after Barbara passed on, to help oot. It was a sad business. John threw himself into work on the farm and didnae have much time for the boys.' Flora paused, then added, 'He needs to find himself another wife.'

Hugh and Maggie looked at each other, while the other members of the family glanced at their mother and then looked down at the table. Flora noticed the uncomfortable looks on their faces.

'Well, the boys need a mither. Wee James is only three years old and a hired woman is no mither,' Flora added, as way of an explanation for her earlier, somewhat unsympathetic, remark.

'Aye. You're probably right, but ye ken how he was devoted to Barbara, it's only twa years since she died,' Hugh added. There was another embarrassed silence around the table. Maggie decided to change the topic of discussion.

'Well, we will be going doon there soon to visit them. It'll be nice to see the twa laddies.'

'How are things up at Birnieknowe Row?' Flora asked Maggie, continuing with the changes in the conversation. Flora asked, because Maggie grew up at Birnieknowe and her family still lived close to the farm.

'Well Grandmither is still wie us. She's ninety-three this year and as tough as a highland steer. She's lives with my aunt,' Maggie replied. 'Mither looks like she is going to follow her ain mither and live to her nineties. She still has quite a hoose full. My brothers are still living there. They work doon the pits. So, it was guid to see the family.'

'Aye. I'm sure that Tom wid like another laddie though,' Hugh added

'Well, he's just got to take what the guid Lord gies him,' Flora proclaimed.

Maggie continued with her summary of her family members and their business.

'My uncle Robert is working on Birnieknowe farm just now. His lads are doon the pits as well, so I dinnae get to see them.'

'There's a lot of folks that dinnae see much of the sunlight through working doon the pits. Yer uncle Rob is lucky to be working at the farm. I ken oor Tom values his work,' Hugh observed.

'I get to meet quite a few men in Manitoba who used to work doon the pits and hae managed to escape,' Hugh added. 'They think that they hae reached paradise when the get oot to the prairies with all the fresh air and sunlight.'

Gilbert had come into the farm house quietly, without anyone noticing. He had been listening to the conversation and felt compelled to add his own comment.

'Aye. I ken how they must feel, Hugh. That's just what I want to do.' Gilbert looked pointedly at his mother.

'Ye get plenty of fresh air and sunlight working here Gilbert. Ye dinnae need to go to Canada to find it,' Flora asserted.

Hugh looked sympathetically at Gilbert. He knew that Gilbert was desperate to return to Canada for a longer spell. He would speak to his mother and try and persuade her to let Gilbert come back with them when they returned.

***

The glow in the eastern sky from the rising sun was getting brighter each morning as John stirred from another restless night's sleep. He had woken again in the bed that was too big for him. Every morning he turned to look at the side of the bed where Barbara used to smile at him and make his heart melt. He still felt her loss, even though it had been two years since he held her hand as she slipped away from him and her two sons. At last spring seemed to be awakening at Balladoyle, with the promise of rich grass, healthy calves and a good harvest.

As he dressed to go out to start the milking, he heard James, his younger son, cry out from his bedroom. James was too young to miss his mother for long, but wee John had only recently stopped looking for her around the house. He had hired a housekeeper to look after the boys and take charge of the house affairs, but she did not show much affection for the boys and he knew that he should remarry at some time. He pondered on the young woman who he had met towards the end of the previous year, at a farm gathering in Dumfrieshire. Her father farmed just across the border into England at a farm called the Riddings, near Canonbie. She had caught John's attention and was a pleasant young woman. Perhaps he would call on her again soon. His thoughts were broken by the sound of yet another rain shower on the bedroom window pane.

'Is it ever going to stop raining?' he thought to himself. He would need to go to the beach and collect more pebbles to put in the gateways so that the cows did not get too muddy. It took a long time for the water to drain from the low-lying land that made up the farm, so it was a constant battle to keep gateways clear of mud. He made his way downstairs to the kitchen where Mary Bell, the housemaid, was busy getting the stove lit to make breakfast.

'Guid marning, Mary. I hope that ye slept well,' John enquired.

'Aye. Thank you, Mr Baird. As well as could be expected,' Mary replied.

John smiled at her reply. He knew that Mary shared a bedroom with Maggie McMinn, the second maid, who snored loudly. However, he knew that Maggie had been asked for her hand in marriage, so it was likely that she would be leaving at the next hiring fair. As John made his way out into the yard and down the lane to the field, where the cows were waiting to come in to the parlour he mused again on the other Mary Bell, the attractive young farmer's daughter from the Riddings, and whether he should make more effort to visit her and see if she would welcome his interest in her.

Later that morning wee John and James were playing in the garden. The rain had eventually cleared and the sun broken through the clouds. Wee John was thirsty after running around so he made his way into the kitchen to get some water. Mrs Campbell, the housekeeper, was giving out orders at the housemaids. Nothing that they did ever seemed to meet her satisfaction. She spotted John coming into the kitchen.

'And what do you want?' she barked.

'I want a drink of water,' wee John replied.

'Well, you can just go out. We are too busy to give you water,' she snapped.

John stood looking at her back as he pondered what to do. He was so thirsty. Perhaps he could find some water in the dairy, he thought. As he turned to leave the kitchen, he saw the jug of milk that was left over from breakfast. Standing on his tip-toes he reached over and pulled the jug towards him. He manoeuvred the jug so that the spout was towards him and then tipped the jug so that some milk poured into his mouth. It splashed into his mouth and down the front of his shirt.

'What do you think you are doing, you little devil?' Janet Campbell shouted.

John nearly tipped the jug off the table at the sudden noise from behind him.

'So, you want some milk do you? Well let me help you,' She said sarcastically.

She grabbed hold of the back of wee John's shirt and then lifted the jug towards his mouth.

'Open yer mouth then,' she ordered. She then started to pour milk into wee John's mouth. He desperately tried to swallow it down and breath. He found himself choking and tried to pull away from the stream of white liquid that was filling his mouth. In the end he coughed and spluttered the milk onto the floor and gasped a breath.

'Come on, if you want milk so badly you can drink more than that.' Janet Campbell grabbed wee John's head and pulled it back to pour yet more milk into his mouth. Wee John was getting frightened now, he tried to gulp the milk down while he held his breath, but eventually he got to the stage when he had to breathe so he pushed out with his hands on the table to get away from the jug and the stream of milk. Janet Campbell released her grip and pushed him toward the door.

'Don't ever come in here and try to steal food again,' she commanded.

Wee John ran out of the kitchen back to the garden outside in tears, wiping the milk from his face. He missed his mother even more.

The scene in the kitchen was witnessed by Mary, the maid. Mary was as frightened of Mrs Campbell as the two wee boys. She wanted to tell John what was going on when he was not in the house, but couldn't think of how to do this without getting herself into trouble with Mrs Campbell. She knew Catherine Wright, who had the farm close to Balladoyle, as Catherine was her mother's cousin. She decided that she would confide in Catherine to see if some message could be passed onto John. So, a week later, when it was her afternoon away from the farm, she walked over to Catherine Wright's farm and knocked on the door. The dogs had been barking long before she reached the door, so it was opened almost immediately by Catherine.

'Hello. It's Mary isn't it? I've seen you walk down the road a few times to Balladoyle. How can I help you?' she asked.

'I wonder if I could speak to ye about something. I've been at a loss as to who I can approach and I remembered visiting here with ma a few years ago.' Mary spoke nervously.

'Aye. Come on in. I'll get the kettle on,' Catherine responded in a kindly, welcoming manner.

They settled in the parlour and Mary explained the reason for her visit. Catherine listened carefully and with some consternation. She had wondered how the Baird boys were faring after Barbara had passed away. She had offered help to John soon after her death and although John was always as polite and friendly when they met at the church or in town, he had not asked for any help. She was sad to hear that the boys were not being treated kindly.

'To be honest, Mrs Wright, I am frightened of Mrs Campbell and fear that she would try to get rid of me if I spoke to Mr Baird myself. I was hoping that you might be able to say something to Mr Baird to let him know how his boys are being badly treated. The wee lads cannie speak for themselves,' Mary confided, her voice dropping to a whisper.

'You've done the right thing, Mary, coming to me. I will find the right time to speak to Mr Baird and see if we can put things right. You go back to the farm and do what you can to look after the boys.' Catherine Wright assured Mary. She reached forward and clasped Mary's hands, which she had been rubbing over each other in nervousness.

'And dinnae fret.'

***

John and his sons arrived at church, as they did every Sunday, in their best clothes. Catherine Wright saw them walking along in front of her towards the Church of Scotland. She had planned what she would say to John about what she had heard from Mary. Then she spotted Mrs Campbell hurrying along the pavement to catch up with John and the boys. She was not expecting her presence. This would make it much more difficult to speak to John without arousing suspicions. She followed the congregation as the filed into the church, greeting various people who she recognised. She sat a couple of rows back from the Bairds and thought about how she was going to speak to John.

The service continued and eventually it finished and the minister was at the door ready to greet the departing members of his flock. Catherine shuffled along the pew in order to get behind John as he left the church. But by the time she left the church herself John was engaged in conversation with another farmer. Catherine could hear his booming voice. She hovered around the group hoping to catch his eye, but was approached herself by a friend who engaged her in conversation and when she turned to look in John's direction, she saw that John was walking towards the road. She excused herself and hurried after John.

'Mr Baird,' she called after him.

'Good morning, Mrs Wright,' John answered. 'I hope that ye are well.'

'Aye. I was hoping to catch ye afore ye left for Balladoyle. I wanted to have a word about some troubling information that I have been told.'

'Oh?' John responded.

Catherine saw Janet Campbell at the church gates, holding the boys' hands and looking back at her and John. She wondered whether to wait until another time, but John was already standing looking at her and waiting himself.

'Ye had better just come oot with it then.'

'Aye. I'll just come out with it,' she stated as boldly as possible. 'I've been told by someone, who I dinnae want to name, that yer Mrs Campbell is very hard on yer boys. Harder than she needs to be. They are such sweet laddies. I wouldn't want them to suffer in the way that it has been described to me.'

John looked at Catherine to try and judge whether there was any alternative reason for passing on the information. However, as far as he knew there was no animosity between his housekeeper and Catherine Wright.

'That's interesting information Mrs Wright. I will bear that in mind and ensure that discipline and kindness are dispense fairly and equally. I dinnae want the laddies to suffer either.' He turned to look down the road where Janet Campbell was waiting for John to join them. 'Thank ye, Mrs Wright. I appreciate that it must have been difficult for ye to broach this to me. As I said, I'll mind what ye have told me.' He touched his cap and walked on thoughtfully. Perhaps it was time to speed up his plans to court John Bell's daughter, Mary, and get a permanent solution to the upbringing of his sons.

***

Back at Garclaugh, Hugh had finally decided to tackle his mother about Gilbert being allowed to travel out to Canada with him and Maggie and the family when they returned in mid-March.

'You cannae keep him at Garclaugh. He's a man now, he can make his ain decisions,' Hugh reasoned to his mother.

'And how is Andrew to manage the farm when he gets poorly?' Flora declared.

'Andrew can hire men to do the heavy work. Gilbert is no the only man who can lift a bag of corn,' Hugh continued with his argument.

'Aye, but Andrew needs someone who he can trust, not some *here today, gone tomorrow* hired man,' Flora insisted.

'There are plenty of trustworthy men who I can hire to help oot on the farm.' The voice of Andrew projected through from the back place, where he had entered from the yard, unheard by Hugh or Flora. He walked through to join Hugh and Flora.

'The last thing I want to do is to trap a resentful Gilbert on the farm. If he wants to go to Canada, then for the Lord's sake let him go. He's no a laddie anymore, Mither. Ye cannae keep him tied to yer apron.'

Silence descended on the kitchen, as Flora took in what Andrew had said.

'Ah well. There's clearly nae more that I can say, is there? If he is determined to join you in Canada, I better help him with some money to pay for his passage and things.'

Hugh and Andrew glanced at each other and smiled, with a look of victory on their faces. At last, they had won an argument with their stubborn mother. Later that afternoon Hugh caught up with Gilbert, as he came in from the fields with some horses, to tell him that Flora had at last given way and would help him pay for his passage across to Canada. So, on 14 March Hugh, Gilbert, Maggie and the children, John, Alex and wee Maggie, left Glasgow for the port of St John, on the east coast of Canada.

***

As the group left Glasgow to travel to Canada, John left Balladoyle and took the train to Carlisle and then the Waverley line towards Edinburgh. However, not far north of Carlisle John left the train at Riddings Junction, from where it was a short walk to Riddings Farm, the home of John Bell and his wife Janet. This was the home of Mary Ellen Bell, the young woman whom John had met previously and whom he wanted to meet again. He had sent a telegram to the Bell household, so that he was expected.

The Riddings Farm was a dairy farm and was situated close to where the River Esk met Liddel Water, right on the Scotland–England border. The Waverley railway line went through the farm, so the sound and sight of trains on their journey between Carlisle and Edinburgh was a regular feature of life on the farm. There was also another line that branched off at the station and went across the river towards Langholm, so although the station at Riddings Junction seemed to be in the middle of nowhere, there were always passengers embarking and disembarking at the two platforms as they swopped trains.

John Bell greeted John Baird at the steps of the farm house.

'Good day, John. We are so glad that you could visit us. We don't get many visitors here, despite the railway line taking thousands through our farm every day,' he replied in a jolly manner.

John had arrived in time for the lunch, so he soon seated at a large table surrounded by the Bell family. John found himself next to the eldest son, Robert, who was keen to talk to John about Ayrshire cattle, as they had used one of the Garclaugh bulls. John, however, wanted to talk with Mary, who had been seated opposite John. Eventually Janet Bell could see that Robert's cow conversation was distracting John from his main intention for visiting the Bells.

'Wheesht Robert, don't talk about cows all the time. We get enough talk about cows at the dinner table,' Janet scolded.

John decided to break the silence that followed Janet Bell's admonishment.

'So, ye must border Scotland here. It's just ower the river no doubt,' he asked.

'Aye, you could see Scotland over the river. Although there is a wee bit of Scotland on this side of the river. When they were building the Waverley line the route that they planned wouldn't fit along the river bank, so they had to either move the route or move the river. They decided it was cheaper to move the river and so they dug a new route for the river and filled in the old river bed for the railway line. So, there is about two acres of land on this side of the river that is Scotland,' John Bell explained.

'That would have been enough to start a war in the auld days,' John Baird added with a chuckle.

'You may not know that we have plans to move down your way

fairly soon. We are planning to take on a farm at Aspatria,' John Bell commented.

'Is that so,' John replied thoughtfully. This would mean that Mary would be closer to Balladoyle and easier to visit.

'Aye, it's a fair-size place called Warwick Hall. If we get the lease all sorted, then we would hope to move in about three months' time. Perhaps we may be up and look at some of your cattle.'

After lunch John took a walk with Mary down to the railway line and then across to Liddel Water. They talked for quite a while before John pulled his watch out from his waistcoat pocket and announced that he would have to catch the train back to Silloth in order to get the milking started. Mary was a dairy farmer's daughter and knew the demands of milking. They walked back to the farm house and John gave his farewells and thanks to the Bell family before making his way back to Balladoyle. He had made his mind up that he would ask Mary for her hand in marriage, but he would need to make sure that she was as willing as he was about his intentions. He would wait until the Bell family were settled properly at their new farm at Aspatria before he would approach Mary's father.

***

Back at Balladoyle John kept a careful eye on what was happening in the house. Janet Campbell was aware of the extra scrutiny and was careful to put on a show of motherliness to the boys whenever John was around. She suspected that one of the maids had told John something that had made him suspicious, so she turned her venom on the maids instead. John had come in for some breakfast after the milking and was reading the newspaper from the previous day.

'Is there any interesting news, Mr Baird?' Janet Campbell asked John.

'No, not much. The usual rumbles aboot war in Europe. Everyone seems worried that Germany is sabre rattling wie its neighbours and itching to start a war,' John replied.

'Isn't the Kaiser a grandson of Queen Victoria?' Janet Campbell asked.

'Most of the royal families in Europe are descendants of Queen Victoria.' John chuckled. 'She married off her daughters to any royal prince that was available.'

'If they are all related, why can't they just sort out their problems without going to war?'

'That's why they are likely to go to war, because they are all related!' John exclaimed. 'Have you ever seen a family that doesn't have a row going on at some time?'

It was only a couple of weeks later that the assassination of Archduke Franz Ferdinand took place in Sarajevo, followed a month later by the sound of young men cheering in the streets to the news that war had been declared between Britain and Germany. Although Britain ruled the waves with the largest navy in the world, its land forces were small by comparison with Germany, leading to the Kaiser supposedly calling the British Expeditionary Force that was sent across the English Channel 'that contemptible little army'.

***

News of the war in Europe filled the newspapers that reached Hugh in McAuley. Canada, like all of Britain's colonies, joined the war with Germany at the same time that Britain declared. The Baird family gathered for their evening meal, while Hugh read out the highlights from the newspaper that he held.

> *'Facing twice the number of German troops the British Expeditionary Force gallantly fought and defeated German forces at the Battle of Mons. Despite this success they withdrew in order to provide support for the retreating French Fifth Army,'* Hugh read out.

'I tell ye. This war will be ower by Christmas. The Germans have got the Russians pushing into Prussia from the East and the French, Belgians and British from the West. I cannae see how they will be able to overcome oor professional British army,' Hugh proclaimed.

'Now that Canada has declared war on Germany as well, I wonder if the Canadian army will go ower there?' Gilbert asked.

'I am sure that the Canadian generals will be keen to get their new army stuck into a proper war,' Hugh responded. 'God help all those young soldiers who will be sent ower there.'

'Why do all you men get so excited aboot a war? Young men will die, like in every war. Then years later people will ask why they had to die,' Maggie added. 'Now sit yerselves doon for yer supper.'

CHAPTER 8
1915

❧⧫☙

The year 1914 drifted into 1915 with reports of victories and set-backs in the war raging across northern Europe. The British Expeditionary Force were almost entirely wiped out at the First Battle of Ypres, so new, young, inexperienced volunteers were shipped over to replace them. There was no shortage of volunteers, as young men all over Britain stood in recruitment lines, determined to escape the drudgery of their lives down coal mines or in hot, smoky and dirty factories. The excitement of being a soldier was a great attraction for a young man with no prospects.

A large Canadian Expeditionary Force voyaged across the Atlantic and took part in their first action at the Second Battle of Ypres in April 1915, where they were exposed to the horrors of modern warfare, when chlorine gas was used by the Germans. The French forces, stationed adjacent to the Canadians, bore the brunt of the gas attack, so the Canadians found themselves having to stop the German advance through the gaps created in French lines by the chlorine. The excitement of being a soldier wore off very quickly.

Gilbert only read about these battles in the newspapers, but he was starting to feel that he should be doing something to help out. He felt like a Canadian and had told the census recorders that visited the farm the previous summer that he was a naturalised Canadian, although he had never officially signed any naturalisation documents. For the time being he was required to work on the farm and produce food for the troops in Europe, although more and more posters appeared in McAuley encouraging young men to join their uniformed peers.

***

The United States were not involved in the European war, so life progressed as previously. Percy Roberts was busy building his

Penhurst herd of Ayrshire cows, many of which were descendants of Garclaugh cows and bulls. But the pride of his herd was a very white Ayrshire cow called May Mischief, which he had bought at great expense from Andrew Baird five years earlier. May Mischief had been worth every dollar that he had spent. She produced prodigious amounts of milk, so that during 1915 she was recorded as having produced 2945 gallons of milk, which was declared as a world record. Percy Roberts was more than happy to advertise this achievement and immediately sent a telegram to Andrew at Garclaugh.

Andrew was walking across the yard at Garclaugh when the uniformed postman came down the drive on his bike. The bike slid to a stop in front of Andrew.

'Guid marning, Mr Baird. I hae a telegram for ye,' the postie announced.

Andrew signed for the telegram then made his way into the farmhouse.

'Is that the postie I saw coming doon the drive Andrew?' Flora asked.

'Aye. I have a telegram from America,' Andrew replied, in a puzzled manner.

He opened the telegram and read the contents. When he finished reading, he lowered his arm and stared ahead in thought. Then Flora saw a smile creep onto his face.

'Well? What's the telegram say?' she asked impatiently.

'It's May Mischief. The coo that I sold to that Mr Roberts. She's been declared a world champion for the amount of milk that she produced in a year.'

'Well! World champion. That's some achievement. Yer faither wud be so proud of ye, Andrew. Does he say how much milk she produced?' Flora asked.

Andrew looked back at the telegram. 'No. I expect that he will write to me with more details. Fancy that, a Garclaugh coo is the world champion. I'll have to charge more for the use of my bulls now. Perhaps that deserves a wee dram,' he stated, moving towards the cabinet that held his bottle of whiskey.

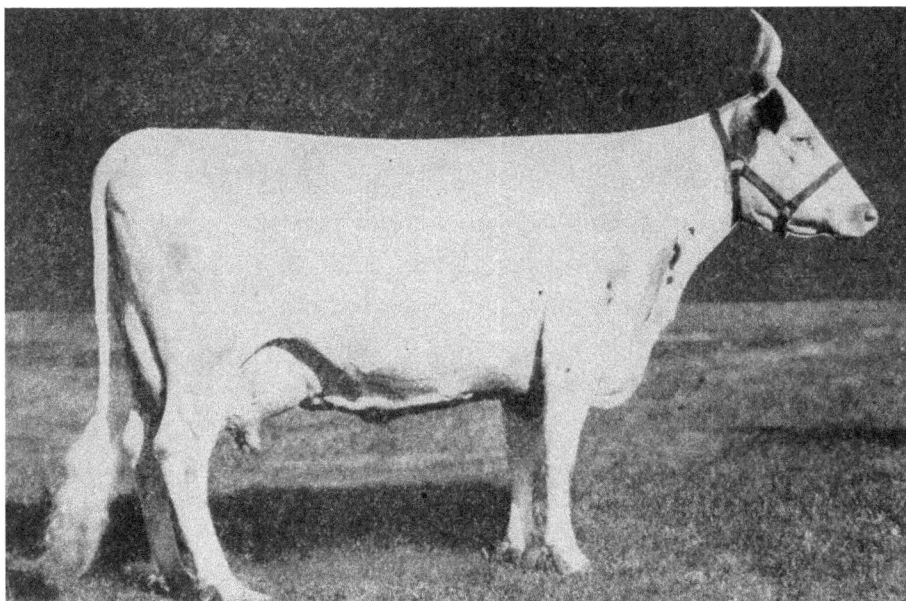

May Mischief.

***

News of May Mischief being declared a world champion soon reached Balladoyle, where John's schoolfriend Mungo Sloan was visiting.

'Ye'll hae to put a sign up on the road telling folk that you hae kye from the same herd as the world champion,' Mungo teased John.

'Aye, well. Perhaps I will,' John retorted.

Mungo and John were leaning on the field gate, in the summer sunshine, looking across at his herd of Ayrshires cows. Two dairy farmers would always find plenty of conversation about cows, milk and cheese, but there were other events that came to mind on this day.

'So, you didn't have any bother getting past the scene of the railway disaster at Gretna?' John asked Mungo.

'No. They must have cleared a lot of the wrecked carriages quite quickly to get the line reopened. As we went through the junction the burnt-out carriages and mangled engines were still heaped on either side of the track. There was sombre mood in the carriages knowing that 230 soldiers lost their lives in the fires. You could still smell the smoke, as the remains of some of the wooden carriages were still smouldering,' Mungo replied.

'A dreadful, dreadful event. Five trains involved in yen accident. Those poor young soldiers on their way to the war, not thinking that they would lose their lives in their ain country,' John mused. He had already enquired at the local recruiting office about signing up for the army, but they had told him that he was needed more on his farm providing food and horses for the soldiers overseas.

On 22 May 1915 three trains converged on a loop junction that allowed one train to overtake another. Two trains were waiting on side loops while faster trains were coming up and down the main line close to Carlisle. A troop train collided with the back of a stationary goods train, then a fast express going the opposite direction ploughed into the wreckage from the first accident. Gas on the express train exploded causing the wooden carriages packed with soldiers on their way to the war to catch alight, incinerating 230 soldiers and civilians. An inquest, followed by a court trial, eventually blamed Britain's worst train accident on two of the signal operators.

'Wars used to be between armies on other continents, but this one is now affecting civilians over here. I got a letter from Barbara's brother in Southend the other day. A zeppelin airship dropped bombs on Southend and some fell not so far away from their hoose,' John explained.

'Aye John, I read aboot the raid in the paper. There was a fair bit of damage from these incendiary bombs that they dropped and I seem to remember that there was a lady got killed,' Mungo replied.

'What do the Germans think will happen when they drop bombs on civilians? What with the Lusitania being sunk and all these reports of German atrocities, all it did was encourage more men to sign up to be soldiers,' John continued. 'Anyways, Barbara's brother David was writing aboot the night raid. They were wakened in the night by these bangs and what sounded like rifle fire. They were used to the anti-aircraft guns just ootside of the town practicing, but not at three o'clock in the morning. When David looked oot of his bedroom window, he could see the glow of a fire in a house a few streets away and then he looked up and saw the zeppelin up in the sky. As he watched he heard more bombs exploding and more fires. He was writing that they all got very scared that one might hit their hoose.'

'I'm no surprised they were scared,' Mungo responded. 'Where could you run when there were bombs come down from the sky?'

As John and Mungo talked about the zeppelin raid, their conversation was interrupted by a loud booming noise coming from the direction of the Solway Firth.

'Good heavens, John,' Mungo exclaimed. 'That was some bang. Do ye get many like that?'

'Aye. When the battery is testing some new shell or some new gun, we get bangs like that regularly throughout the day, sometimes for several days. Then Armstrongs will be testing some other gun and it will take them a week or so to bring in all the new equipment by the railway, so we might go for quite a while without hearing anything. Obviously since the war started, testing has increased tremendously,' John explained.

The Blitterlees Battery was set up within the sand dunes on the Solway Firth by armaments company Armstrong Whitworth in 1886 in order to test their long-range large guns. The relatively unpopulated area meant that the noise would disturb few people, but the huge expanse of sand exposed at low tide also provided easy access for the retrieval of the remains of the shells. When the war broke out, the War Ministry made use of the testing range, as well as Armstrong Whitworth. A railway line had been constructed off the main line to allow special trains to take the guns and ammunition to the testing site.

Gun testing at Blitterlees battery.

'So have the ministry taken any of yer horses yet, John?' Mungo asked.

'No, not yet. We had some official came around last month to register what horses we had and what horses we needed. He said that we should start breeding more horses, as they would be needed for the war. Sounds like a good venture. I dinnae ken how much they will be paying, but it won't be top prices,' John noted.

'As lang as they don't start taking oor best breeding stock. I hae some old yens that they can have. It will save me having to tak them to the knackers yard.' Mungo chuckled.

'One of my men decided to sign up last week. So, he will be off fairly soon. It may be true that Your Country Needs You, as Lord Kitchener's posters tells us, but oor farms need them as well,' John mused.

The two friends pondered in silence on how the war was affecting their farming. Mungo broke the silence.

'So, everything is sorted for the wedding?' Mungo asked.

'Aye, I think so. It seems a way off yet, but it will be here soon,' John replied

'Mary is a lovely lass and the boys seem to have warmed to her.'

'It will be good to try and get the family settled. I had to get rid of the housekeeper, Campbell. I found that she had been hitting wee John. All children need discipline, but the only thing that they will learn from unreasonable beatings is violence,' John stated.

There was another period of silence. The silence that feels comfortable between friends.

'So, have ye heard anything from yer brother Gilbert oot in Canada? How's he getting on oot there?' Mungo asked.

'Mither gets letters from him occasionally. He hasn't contacted me since he went oot there. I widnae be at all surprised if he stays oot there. There's not much over here for him. I can't imagine that he wid want to work for Andrew at Garclaugh again, or for Tom at Birnieknowe,' John mused.

Mungo and John wandered back to the farmhouse, as wee John and James came running out of the garden towards them.

'Pa, pa,' James shouted. 'John's got a big spider.'

James ran to his father who swept him up into his protective arms.

'It's no a real spider, Pa,' wee John explained. 'It's just a piece of moss that I am pretending is a spider.'

'Go and get yerselves washed for supper. It's sausages tonight.' John told the boys, as he put James back down onto the ground and watched them race off towards the rain butt to wash their hands.

'You and Mary are going to hae yer hands full with those two.' Mungo chuckled.

'Aye, but it will be a pleasure watching them grow up. They will do Barbara proud,' John remarked.

***

John and Mary Bell were married on 23 November at the Aspatria Congregational Church. Mary's brother John had taken up the lease on Warwick Hall farm at Aspatria and Mary had moved down to help her brother on the farm, as well as be closer to her intended husband at Balladoyle, just fifteen miles to the north. The weather was exceptionally cold with temperatures having dropped well below zero since the middle of November. The Bell family lit big fires at Warwick Hall as they welcomed the wedding guests back for a hot meal and plenty of whiskey. John Baird's brother, Tom, had accompanied their mother Flora and Chrissie to the wedding, but Andrew was not well enough to travel and sister Mary did not cope well with large crowds.

Although it was a wedding, much of the conversation amongst the guests was about the war and deaths that had occurred with local families. Pressure was being put on the menfolk who had not yet joined up to 'do their duty'. With farmer workers generally being turned away at recruiting stations some resentment had surfaced within the community, with critical comments being directed at farmers and their men. Everyone hoped that the war would soon be over in the new year and that normal life could resume, although many doubted that this would be possible.

CHAPTER 9
1916

꧁꧂

The third year of the war began with news that conscription was being introduced for all men between eighteen and forty years old, with exemption for important occupations, such farming. This announcement, although anticipated, brought protests from many people, not least those factory owners and farmers who relied on young men to carry out the work that was needed. However, women had been recruited to carry out many of the tasks previously carried out by men and also the many jobs that had been created by the demands from the front. Many of these jobs would take place in the huge ammunition towns and factories that were being constructed west of Gretna, on the other side of the Solway Firth to Silloth. The demand for workers, particularly women, brought more pressures on the famers in the area as their workers decided to find more lucrative and exciting employment making cordite for the millions of shells that would be fired across the trenches. The cordite produced was named the *Devil's porridge* by Sir Arthur Conan Doyle, after he visited one of the factories. At its peak over 11000 women and 5000 men produced 800 tonnes of cordite every week. The work, however, caused them many medical problems, as the chemicals were toxic and there was little protective clothing.

The war in Europe had its impact on all the British and German colonies and the trenches of France and Belgium were now populated by soldiers from all over the world. Not only were Canadian soldiers being shipped over to France, but horses were also making the journey across the Atlantic. As in Britain, Canadian farmers were having to give up some of their horses to the war effort. At Mansfield farm in McAuley Hugh was bemoaning the loss of one of his young Clydesdales, which he was hoping to be able to use to replace one of the older ones.

'I offered him the older one, but he said that it was too old and that they only wanted the young, fit ones. I even offered him it at half the usual price, but he just laughed and said that I would have to keep the old yen going for a while longer,' Hugh explained to Gilbert.

'Ye hae got the young colt coming on, he should be ready for heavier work soon,' Gilbert tried to pacify Hugh.

'They'll be taking him if we are not careful. We may need to hide him awa somewhere,' Hugh suggested.

'Ye wouldn't be very popular if they found oot,' Gilbert replied.

'Well, they are no very popular with me and all the farmers are trying avoid their best horses being taken. Some farmers even believe that they would get their horses back after the war. No chance of that happening. The soldiers will most likely eat them,' Hugh pointed out.

'When I was in toon last week some wifie asked me why I was no in uniform,' Gilbert told Hugh.

'What did you say?'

'I said that I hadnae signed up yet,' Gilbert replied.

'So, are ye planning to sign up?' Hugh asked.

'Do ye think I should?'

'It's your decision, no mine.'

'Perhaps I could join the local militia, so that I could continue to work on the farm,' Gilbert suggested.

'Aye. That's yen way of getting into uniform. Perhaps it would stop the looks that you get from the wifies,' Hugh added.

A few weeks later Gilbert joined the local Active Militia. The Active Militias were historic military groups that were formed to defend Canada. As the British army withdrew from Canada, following the war of 1812, the active militias were expanded to provide a uniformed volunteer part-time force. The regiments consisted of farmers and workers, with permanent and fully trained army personnel as their officers. It was from these regiments that the Canadian Expeditionary Force was formed at the outbreak of the war. Having become part of a military unit it was inevitable that Gilbert would then be persuaded to become part of the regular army and begin his training for as a member of the 79th Cameron Highlanders of Canada. He took the oath to serve in the Canadian Over-Seas Expeditionary Force on 6 September 1916.

***

'Gilbert's joined up in Canada,' Andrew read aloud from the letter that he had open in front of him at the kitchen table.

'What do ye mean joined up?' Flora asked.

'Exactly what I said. He's joined the Canadian army. He's a regular soldier now and is likely to be shipped over to France,' Andrew confirmed.

'Well, I wondered which yen of my sons would end up fighting in this war,' Flora responded with an air of resignation. 'Does he say when he will be going over?'

'No. I doubt that he even knows himself,' Andrew replied.

'Aye, well. We will just have to say our prayers for him and all the other young men who are going to a war that seems to have no end. Perhaps it will end when they have run out of men to send over,' Flora mused. 'When I was in town today I saw two young men hobbling down the street with legs missing. Apparently, the Robinson's lad came hame with his face shot away. He spends all his days in their hoose, as he can't abide the horrified looks he gets when people see his face with no nose and scars. The lads get compensation for losing a leg, but nothing for having their faces messed up. Let's hope Gilbert keeps well clear of bullets and bombs.'

'Well, that's not going to be easy for him when he is expected to hold a gun and charge the enemy trenches,' Andrew replied.

Andrew heaved himself out of his chair. His pernicious anaemia was getting worse and he was struggling with fatigue and shortness of breath. He stood for a while until his dizziness dispersed then he made his way to the back place and out into the yard to see his precious herd of Ayrshires. Flora watched him as he slowly walked across the yard.

'I don't know how he manages to keep going. Poor laddie.' Flora spoke partly to herself and partly to Mary who was busy at the range with some cooking. Mary looked across at her mother, but did not reply. Since the trauma that she suffered when she woke up during a hospital operation, she became a shadow around the house, barely speaking. Chrissie came along the passage from the front room.

'What was that you were saying ma?' she asked.

'Oh, nothing really. I was just watching Andrew struggling to get around and wondering how much longer he will be able to keep going.

All these medicines that Dr Richardson keeps suggesting don't seem to make much differences. John was saying that he is starting to get some of the same symptoms as well, so it seems to be a Baird problem,' Flora responded mournfully to Chrissie.

'Aye. Andrew certainly has a Baird problem. He doesn't know how to sit down and tak a rest,' Chrissie mused, as she looked through the kitchen window as Andrew went into one of the calf pens. 'I wouldn't be at all surprised if announces yen day that he is engaged to be married to yen of his kye.'

'Well, that's probably as close as he will get to a marriage,' Flora replied.

There was a grunting noise coming from the front room.

'That's Will. He doesn't like being left on his own. I will go and read him a story,' Chrissie told Flora.

William was born mentally affected and had spent the past thirty years confined to the farmhouse. Although he was not capable of feeding himself and had limited mobility, the family acknowledged when he was quite young that he was aware of his surroundings and that he responded to family members. They assumed that he could not understand the stories that were being read to him, but he always relaxed when a story was being read and appeared to be listening. Flora and John were determined that he would not go to an institution, so over the years they hired a long succession of maids to help look after him. Both Mary and Chrissie shared this workload. He was a big man and was not easy to move around, so sometimes they were both needed to get him into the bed that was set up in the small room on the ground floor.

CHAPTER 10
1917

❧

December brought bitterly cold weather to Britain and northern Europe. Following a wet autumn, the sodden fields in Scotland and in Cumberland became thick with ice. Before the milking could start in the byres, fires had to be lit to melt the ice that had formed overnight in pipes and iron buckets. Over in Belgium and France the soldiers in the trenches had limited opportunities to light fires and the ice that covered the wooden walkways and ladders made moving around even more dangerous than usual. Soldiers who looked after the horses chose to sleep in the canvas stables with the horses, in order to benefit from the warmth from the animals themselves.

The cold winter continued into 1917, with one of the longest spells of continuous cold weather for many years. Some soldiers claimed that the constant shelling by both armies was causing the bad weather, however, others laughed at the idea. When the major battle of Arras took place in April the weather was still very cold. British, French and Canadian troops were ordered forward in miserable conditions to attack the Germans front line. After some initial success the attack was beaten back and the battle ended with minimal gains for the Allies and 150,000 dead soldiers. News of the abdication of Tsar Nicholas in Russia confirmed the fears that the Germans could now move troops from their eastern front to reinforce the attacks on the Allied forces in France and Belgium.

***

Across in Halifax, Nova Scotia, Gilbert Baird and hundreds of other soldiers, were lined up on the quayside awaiting to board their transport ship to France. They had arrived by train from Camp Hughes, their training camp, packed tightly together in the carriages. Some of the men laughed and joked, others sat in silence, contemplating what they would find at the end of their long journey. On arrival at the train terminal the shouts of the sergeants could be heard ordering the men off the train. Gilbert and his company hauled down their kitbags from the luggage racks and shuffled along the aisles towards the doors of the carriage. The once-empty station platform was quickly filled with khaki uniforms and milling soldiers all moving towards the exits to the platform and the station. The station was next door to the docks, so as soon as they were outside of the impressively large main building, they were all gathering into their units for the march down to the dock where their ship was waiting. Gilbert was part of the 14th Reserve Battalion for the Queens Own Cameron Highlanders of Canada. With their full kilt dress uniforms, they drew admiring looks from groups of civilians who paused to watch them progress down the road from the station. As they left the main road, that ran parallel to the docks, they turned into a side road that gave a view of the dockside. Gilbert heard gasping and loud muttering, followed by orders from the sergeants calling for silence. The cause of this sudden outburst from the soldiers was the sight of the ship that was to be their home for the next ten days. Gilbert's unit were ordered to halt, so they all had an opportunity to gaze at the huge steel structure that towered above them.

'My God. Is that the ship that is taking us to France?' one of Gilbert's section asked.

'Aye. It's the Olympic. One of the largest liners afloat. It's a sister ship to the Titanic,' another squaddie replied, bringing a chuckle to others around.

'You had better pray that it does not suffer the same fate then,' their sergeant barked at them from behind. 'Now keep yer mouths shut.'

Gilbert stared up at the four funnels that were characteristic of these large trans-Atlantic liners. However, it hardly looked like one of these luxury ships, having been painted with dazzle camouflage. Gone were the sleek, black and white livery of the White Star Line, having been replaced by jagged and curved dark blue bands on a light blue background. The camouflage was considered essential to help confuse German U-boats that hunted the north Atlantic for Allied shipping. The Cunard liner *Lusitania* had been sunk in 1915 by a U-boat off southern Ireland, showing that even the fast-moving liners were vulnerable. The

RMS Olympic with dazzle camouflage, transporting Canadian soldiers

Olympic had been chartered by the Canadian government in 1916 in order to transport troops to the battlefields. The ship could carry 6000 soldiers on each trip.

As Gilbert and his unit were moved closer to the Olympic, he could see that it filled the whole of the pier, in fact it was longer than the pier and its stern projected out into the river. To Gilbert it felt as if he was standing in front of a huge cliff. Several wooden gangplanks led to doorways in the side of the cliff face, along which shuffled lines of soldiers with their kit bags on their shoulders or hugged to their chests. At one end of the liner lorries and carts were unloading cargo, which was being hoisted through large hatchways. The whole quayside seemed to be a mass of soldiers, workmen, horses and lorries. Gilbert soon found himself at the bottom of one the gangplanks being shepherded by military policemen. As he made his way up towards the doorway, he took time to look over the edge of the gangplank to the dark water that lapped between the dock wall and the liner.

There was a table just inside the door at the top of the gangplank, at which sat two administration officers. As he came up to the table one of the officers thrust a card into his hand.

'This tells you where you will find your hammock and where you will be eating your meals. Follow the signs and stay there,' the officer stated without looking at Gilbert.

As Gilbert moved forward, he heard the same instructions being given to the following soldiers. He looked at the card and read what was written.

'Compartment A2; deck D, mess table 74, 1st sitting,' it stated.

Gilbert looked up at the prominent signs in front of him. One pointed to the stairwell to deck D, so he turned to his right and followed the soldier in front. He realised that probably all his section had come up the gangplank with him so would have been given a similar accommodation location on the ship. He looked over at the card that his neighbour, Jim Campbell, was holding and saw that it also said compartment A2, deck D. Jim saw Gilbert reading his card.

'Are we in the same place then, Bairdy?' he asked.

'Aye, looks that way. Here's the stairs up to deck D,' Gilbert replied, pointing his card towards another large sign that gave directions to the upper decks. The two men gingerly made their way up the stairs, which was not easy when you had a kitbag in one hand. On deck D, they followed more signs to compartment A2, which turned out to be a long walk towards the bows of the ship.

Compartment A2 had clearly been some sort of relaxation area on the Olympic when it was in normal civilian service. The area had been converted into sleeping quarters by fixing hammocks to the various steel beams. The hammocks were hung so that they were virtually touching one another and there were no walkways. If you wanted to get to your hammock you had to bend over and duck your head and walk in a crouch position. When Gilbert, Jim and most of the rest of his section entered the compartment it was already quite full of soldiers who were claiming various hammocks.

'Let's get a couple of those next to the bulkhead,' Jim suggested.

The two men made their way between the empty hammocks and under the full ones. Some men had thrown their kitbags into the hammocks in order to claim them and then had made their way back to the stairwell to go up on one of the upper decks. Gilbert and his companion found adjacent hammocks and put their own kitbags in the hammocks. Gilbert looked around at the space.

'Where are we supposed to put oor kit when we are sleeping?' he asked.

'I suppose you put it on the floor underneath, or put it in the hammock with you,' Jim replied.

The noise level increased as small arguments broke out about who was having which hammocks and what was supposed to happen to the kitbags. Arguments ceased when one of the sergeants bellowed for silence.

'Once you have claimed a hammock you can go up on deck. The first sitting for supper is at 17:00 hours. If you miss your sitting then you won't get any food, so make sure that you know where you are going and the time,' the sergeant explained.

Gilbert and Jim pushed their way through the soldiers who were now filling the corridors, some going in and some going out. There were curses and barging as everyone tried to find their way to their designated places on the ship. The two men eventually climbed up the stairs into the sunshine that had now evaporated the clouds. The rail on the dockside of the ship was deep with soldiers leaning over and peering down at the activity. Some soldiers were shouting remarks to women and children who had come to say farewell to their husbands, fathers, brothers and sons. The rail was so far above the level of the docks that the words that were being shouted back and forward were lost in the general hubbub of noise. Gilbert and Jim walked over to the less crowded rail that overlooked the harbour and settlement of Dartmouth on the opposite bank. Gilbert took a cigarette that Jim had offered and the two men leaned on the rail in silence and contemplated the view and their impending journey to France.

***

At a station in Cumberland yet more soldiers were in standing in rows, waiting to board a train to Carlisle. The Border Regiment had been recruiting men around Cumberland during the previous months and had now collected enough men at their base at Workington to fill most of a train that would travel from Carlisle to southern England and to take a ship to northern France.

John had come back from a trip the station, having delivered milk, and stomped into the kitchen where Mary was busy getting breakfast ready for the boys.

'Well, there's yet more men left the farms to go to war. I was talking to Gilbert Hanson at the station and twa of his men have signed up and left. He dinnae ken how he is going to manage the farm now,' John boomed at Mary.

'I'm sure that he will find someone who is willing to work,' Mary suggested, more as a way to placate John's anger than as a genuine suggestion.

'Well one of them is Will Johnston, who is one of the best ploughmen around. Ye cannie just larn ploughing with a horse in a couple of days,' John continued his rant. 'If there are any horses left for ploughing after the army have taken all them as well.'

'Well, they put a lot of pressure on these young men to sign up. I ken yen or twa who have had white feathers thrust into their hands by womenfolk in toon,' Mary explained.

'These women dinnae ken what war is like. Perhaps some of them should go across to France and see what it's like in the trenches, afore they start accusing men of cowardice. The stories that some of the soldiers on leave tell their families are horrible.' John paused in thought. 'I just hope that Gilbert stays safe in France.'

'Have ye heard any more from him?' Mary asked.

'No. Just what Mither has told me,' John replied. 'We don't even ken if he is over there now. Hopefully we will get a letter from him at some stage. Right then, these horses will be wanting fed. Perhaps you twa laddies wud like to come a walk with me oer the fields later?'

Both boys looked up with excited smiles on their faces. Jim quickly tried to shovel the last of his porridge into his mouth.

'You finish yer breakfast first. I'll gie you a shout when I am gaing oot.' John then grabbed his cap and left the house in the same rush of energy with which he entered. Mary sighed as quiet returned to the household.

'Well, that was yer fither boys; into the house, then straight out again,' she told them.

***

Gilbert had not yet reached France, in fact he was still on the ship in Halifax harbour, which was crowded with soldiers waiting to leave. After breakfast they had been mustered by their sergeants and issued life-jackets, that they were told they had to wear at all times, except when they were sleeping. It seemed that most of the soldiers were on deck, as word had spread that departure would be at noon. Sure enough, at noon, the horn on the *Olympic* coughed, then roared, making the air shudder. Longshoremen on tugs shouted to sailors on the ship and ropes were thrown and then hauled into large reels. Bells could be heard as commands were signalled to the engine room. The ship began to rumble into life as two floods of muddy water streamed along the ship's flanks and burst against the harbour wall at its bow. As the liner began to back out a cheer began on deck and moved like a wave across the thousands of troops who crowded the decks waving to family members, friends or just the assembled crowds who has turned up to see 'the old reliable' carry another load of young men to the war in a faraway place.

Despite being so close to Canada, the departure of the *Olympic* was one of the more dangerous sections of her journey, as German U-boats would have been alerted to the time of her departure and could be waiting in the seas close to Halifax. Consequently, the *Olympic* was escorted to the high seas by two cruisers and a high-speed torpedo boat that circled the liner as she made her way eastwards. The *Olympic* was so fast that it was considered less dangerous for the liner to travel at full speed, rather than have to go slower and allow escort ships to keep up. It did, however, have to follow a zig-zag course until it reached the deep ocean, where it could travel at its top speed.

Gilbert and Jim were squeezed onto the rail towards the bows of the liner. They had left Halifax in sunshine, but now fog had rolled down from the hills to the north and the temperature had dropped considerably. The cheering and the excitement that had hailed their departure had long since ended, as the men considered their journey and their final destination.

The soldiers on the *Olympic* had got into some sort of routine as they crossed the northern Atlantic waters. Gilbert and his section had learned to eat their meals quickly, as there was always another section arriving who would have been allocated to the same tables. Thankfully the meals were sufficient to keep everyone well fed, although quite a number of the soldiers could only keep the food down for a short time before their sea-sickness had them running to the toilets. The cold air from the Artic meant that any visit to the decks were short. However, much to the excitement of those who had never travelled across the Atlantic, occasionally they spotted icebergs that had drifted down from Greenland.

They had left Halifax on 28 April, so by 5 May they were able to see the northern coastline of Ireland. Two navy cruisers had arrived to escort the *Olympic* into Liverpool. German U-boats operated in these waters and other navy ships patrolled the coastal waters to try and spot these elusive and deadly enemy. The *Olympic* was to have her own encounter with a U-boat in the following year when it spotted one as it approached the coast of France. The U-boat was preparing to launch torpedoes but had some problem flooding the torpedo tubes. The delay gave time for the *Olympic* to alter course and ram the U-boat as it attempted to dive to safety. The U-boat was badly damaged, but the crew managed to get to life rafts before scuttling the submarine.

It took another day for the *Olympic* to reach the dock at Liverpool and yet another day before Gilbert disembarked with his platoon. Once again, they shuffled their way through crowded docks towards a train that would take them south to Dibgate Camp at Shorncliffe, near Folkestone. Dibgate was one of several transit camps that the Canadian Corps used to prepare their soldiers for the war across in France, from where, on a clear day, the men could see its coastline. They arrived in the late afternoon at Sandling Junction station, where the troop train had halted, and marched up the hill leading up to the camp itself. They were met by various officers from 14th Reserve Battalion who directed the different companies and sections to wooden barrack blocks, that were spread over the large site. Sergeants relayed orders from the officers and made sure that silence and discipline were maintained. Most of the men were exhausted after their journey, others still hungry having eaten little on the voyage. Gilbert's section filed into their barrack block clutching their kitbags to their chests. He saw an empty bed next to Jim Campbell so he claimed it by hoisting his kit bag onto the mattress. The block housed a platoon of three sections, in total thirty men, so there was plenty of noise and bustle as they all found a bed and got settled. The noise quickly abated as the arrival of a senior officer was loudly announced by a corporal and all the soldiers jumped off their beds at stood at attention at the end of their beds.

'I am Major Anderson and your commanding officer while you are in quarantine. You will remain in these quarantine barracks for twenty-eight days and you are not permitted to enter the main camp. You will all undergo a medical examination tomorrow and then you will spend the next weeks getting up to fighting fitness. Your NCOs will take you over to the canteen now, where you can take some supper and a hot drink. Lights out will be at ten o'clock. Corporal, you can dismiss the men when you are ready.' He then turned around and left the block, presumably to repeat the same message in the adjacent blocks. The men were then dismissed in their sections and they hurried across to the canteen to join the queue for a welcome meal.

At five-thirty next morning Gilbert continued to lie in his bunk while the bugler played 'reveille', but he got up very quickly when the sergeant arrived. The barrack block jumped into life and the wooden floors resounded to the earnest steps of men trotting out to the latrines. The sun felt warm and welcoming on his face as he too left the block, having donned his kit and boots ready for a fitness run around the perimeter of the quarantine camp. These fitness runs would become part of their routine at the camp for the next four months, so that by the time they were ready to leave for France they could complete the runs with a sixty-pound pack on their bags and holding a rifle.

The British officers looked upon the Canadian soldiers as keen amateurs, so had insisted that there were proper training and practice sessions. Gilbert and his section learned how to dismantle and clean a rifle, how to kill quickly with a bayonet and, of course, how to shoot accurately. Every day the sound of gun shots could be heard from the shooting ranges, often to the irritation of the townsfolk in Folkestone, four miles away. Gilbert and his chums were keen to explore Folkestone and even get the chance to go up to London, so they were counting off the days to the end of quarantine. Despite the routine of fitness runs and training sessions, they were quite enjoying their life in the camp. They had time to themselves during the day and a variety of sports matches were organised by their NCOs. Gilbert was not a sportsman, curling being the only sport that he had ever enjoyed, but he joined in the football and baseball games as best he could.

While the Canadian troops were being cajoled by their sergeant during yet another fitness run, two hundred miles away, at an aerodrome in Belgium, a squadron of fourteen Gotha bombers were being prepared by their German engineers. This was Battle Squadron 3 of the Army High Command, known as the 'Englandgeshwader', or the England Squadron. The squadron was under the command of Captain Ernst Brandenburg, whose mission was to bomb London. The new Gotha bombers had been recently modified with larger petrol tanks and more bomb space.

At midday on 25 May a squadron of twenty-five planes took off from their base heading for their main target, London. When the bombers reached London, it was shrouded in heavy cloud and the airmen who sat at the front of the plane, with the bombs that they intended to drop by hand on their targets, could see nothing beyond the clouds. So, the squadron had to turn to their secondary target, Folkestone harbour in Kent.

During the evening, after supper, the men at the camp sometimes assembled in the canteen for card games and general conversation. It was a warm early summer evening and the thin clouds that had shrouded the camp for most of the day had dispersed. Gilbert was with Jim Campbell, and another friend called Andrew Hamilton, walking around the site; they barely noticed the sound of aircraft in the distance, as RFC Hawkinge was just outside Folkestone and the sound of aircraft was common. It was only when the first aircraft got closer and louder that their attention was drawn to the approaching Gotha bombers. They flew across the camp and directly above them. The three men stood and stared at the aircraft.

'Aren't those German markings on that plane?' Jim remarked.

'I was thinking that too,' Gilbert replied.

Quite quickly they could see activity in the main camp, with officers running and shouting orders. They then heard their own officers shouting for them to find cover. Gilbert, Jim and Andrew stood still in confusion, until they eventually realised that the camp was under attack. The three ran across the parade ground and crouched under a large tree, as explosions could be heard at the other end of the camp. A group of three more bombers flew across the camp and Gilbert and his friends heard more explosions closer to them. A group of NCOs rushed out with a machine gun which they set up on the field, then scanned the sky for further German planes. Although no more planes appeared over the camp, explosions could be heard further to the east over Folkestone itself.

In Folkestone shoppers were crowding the streets, as it was the Friday before the Whitsun bank holiday and extra food was being sought by wives, mothers and maids. The children who accompanied them stared at the silver birds that had appeared in the sky above them. The first bomb exploded outside Stokes Brothers grocery shop in Tontine Street, where there was a queue of women and children patiently waiting to buy potatoes, which had just been delivered. Sixty-one people were killed by that single bomb dropped on the unsuspecting civilians.

After about twenty minutes the sound of planes and explosions ceased and soldiers began to emerge from behind walls and from beneath trees. The sudden and surprising appearance of the German plane was the main topic of conversation for the rest of the evening. News soon came into camp that Folkestone town centre had been attacked by several German bombers. By the morning further shocking news arrived that there had been many casualties. Prior to the attack the townsfolk had ignored the regular sound of the aircraft and had not taken cover, after all this was the first ever raid by German aircraft on Britain, zeppelin raids having ceased nearly a year before. In total ninety-five people were killed, including seventeen Canadian soldiers at the camp and billeted in the town. The raid made national headlines and increased the resolve of the Canadian soldiers at the Dibgate camp to get over to France and contribute to the defeat of the Hun.

Over breakfast the canteen was a continuing buzz of conversation as the soldiers talked of the raid the previous evening. Gilbert was sitting with Jim Campbell, Andrew Hamilton and Harry McAuley.

'I wonder when we will get over to France and see some action?' Jim asked. 'I am getting fed up of all this fitness training and shooting practice.'

'Don't be in such a hurry to get over to France, Jim. It'll be far more deadly than the training here. The targets fire back in France,' Andrew stated.

'I want to get out of quarantine and up to London. I checked with Major Wilson and it is definitely 6 June that we will be able to join the main camp, so long as there are no contagious illnesses here in quarantine,' Harry informed his friends.

'Why, have you got a contagious disease that you plan to give to some unsuspected girl in London, McAuley?' Jim asked with a wink and a chuckle. The others joined in with the mirth.

'Hey, Bairdy, didn't you tell me that you come from a town called McAuley?' Andrew asked.

'Well, I was born and grew up in Ayrshire, but I have been living with my brother at McAuley,' Gilbert explained.

'And Harry's surname is McAuley. So, is that a coincidence or is there a connection?'

'My uncle is George McAuley. When the Canadian Pacific Railway put the railway through Manitoba it went straight through my uncle's farm. So, when they decided to build a station where there were a few cottages, they named the station McAuley. Eventually, a settlement grew around the station and became McAuley village. So, the village was named after my uncle,' Harry explained, with a proud grin.

'I had never heard that story.' Gilbert said. 'I just thought that your uncle named the settlement after himself, not that it was the railway company.'

'Right men. Finish your food and get kitted out for another day's training. You are going to be learning how to dig trenches today.' Sergeant Lewis announced to the canteen, to an anticipated groan.

Following the raid by the German planes it was decided that proper shelter trenches were needed around the site, in case there was another raid. This was not to be their only day of digging trenches; after they had been released from quarantine and moved to the main camp they would spend many days up on the Tolsford Hill digging zig-zag trenches of the type that they might have to dig in France. Throughout the summer they took part in mock attacks, learning to cut their way through barbed wire, crawling across the ground under live shots being fired by a mock enemy. By the beginning of September, they were a fitter and much more efficient fighting force.

Many of the soldiers would write home about the pleasant time that they had at the camp and how much they enjoyed their trips to London when they were given leave. All the vigorous training, of course, was to prepare them for warfare. Warfare that they were soon to experience, as on 12 September the 14th Reserve Battalion were ordered to pack ready to board the trains that would take them to the dock at Folkestone and the ship that would take them over the Channel to Calais.

***

Gilbert had, of course, written to his family back in Ayrshire. The occasional leave that they had been given did not provide sufficient time for Gilbert to travel back to Garclaugh, so they had to rely on an exchange of letters. Flora had just finished reading one of the letters to Andrew, Mary and Chrissie.

'Bye, he seems to be having an exciting time doon south. Fancy the German planes come ower and dropping bombs on Folkestone. The war seems to have come across the water to Britain,' Flora mused. 'I wonder when he will be going over the water to France.'

'He probably won't be told until the day before,' Andrew responded. 'From what he told us in his letters he will certainly be well prepared. All those ditches that we used to have to dig oot around the farm would have given him plenty of training for trench digging. I expect that he would have helped oot the townies who didn't know how to hold a spade properly.'

'Let's hope that he keeps his head doon and comes hame safe,' Chrissie added.

'Aye well, he's not one for needlessly putting himself in harm's way. He's a sensible laddie,' Flora replied, with an anxious thought of the battlefields that she had read about in the papers. She decided to change the subject of their blether.

'So, Chrissie, will be seeing yer young man this weekend?' Flora asked.

'I dinnae ken. He didnae say that he wud be visiting,' Chrissie replied in an embarrassed tone.

John Todd, who was working at Blackwood Farm across the River Nith from Garclaugh, had been courting Chrissie for a few months and it was clear that a relationship was growing. Flora knew the family and she was keen to see her youngest daughter married, although John was ten years younger than Chrissie. Chrissie was an important member of the dairy team and worked alongside Mary in the byre milking the cows. She could also be seen out in the fields helping to cut and collect hay. She would be missed around the farm if the relationship were to develop into a marriage. Good farm workers were not easy to find during the war, when all the young able-bodied men were being called up to fight. Horses were also being conscripted for the war and all British farms were now breeding horses for haulage work in France. The army base where Gilbert spent the summer had extensive stabling for horses, that would be shipped across the Channel, along with the soldiers.

Tractors had been developed in the early years of the Twentieth Century, but they were expensive and unreliable. The war sped up their development and large petrol haulage tractors had also started to be used to move artillery and other heavy loads close to the battle fronts. But it would be many years before they would become a familiar sight on British farms. In the meantime, farmers relied on their Clydesdale horses to move wagons and plough fields, and their daughters to learn how to look after and handle these large animals. Chrissie was certainly up to the task and the horses at Garclaugh knew who was in charge when she took hold of the reins.

***

Gilbert and the rest of the 14th Reserve Battalion arrived in France in September and were immediately loaded onto trains for the journey closer to the front lines. The port at Calais was a bustle of activity as ships unloaded equipment, armaments and horses. Gilbert noted that the unloading work was being carried out by many Chinese labourers and was shocked to see a British officer shouting at one group and beating one of them with a stick. It was clear that some of his unit were equally shocked and he heard mutters of disapproval. While they were waiting to board their train, Gilbert also saw wounded soldiers being carried to a hospital ship on stretchers, as other bandaged casualties followed on crutches.

The insides of the train carriages were very spartan. The carriages were clearly converted freight wagons with wooden benches running down the sides and down the centre. The windows were narrow and most had no glass, which at least meant that there was fresh air. The men settled down for their journey, some smoked, some told jokes and laughed to hide their nervousness. Other men seemed unfazed by the whole experience and even tried to sleep. Gilbert was not one of those men. He sat quietly, with his kit bag between his legs, squeezed between a couple of his unit that he did not know very well. His friend Jim Campbell sat on a middle bench a few places away, but they did not exchange much conversation.

After about two hours the train squealed and shuddered to a halt. Gilbert turned to look out through the slot between the wooden boards that formed the window. He could only see fields, clumps of trees and not much else. The carriage door slid open a little and an officer outside shouted orders for Gilbert's company to disembark. The carriage was quickly filled with shuffling soldiers as they moved towards the double doors that had been pushed fully open, allowing bright sunlight to fill the carriage and make everyone shade their eyes. They jumped down beside the railway tracks, as there was no platform, and followed their sergeant's directions to line up on a road that ran alongside the railway. Eventually it seemed that everyone had disembarked and the NCOs shouted out names from a clipboard, to ensure that all the men that were supposed to be on the train were now lined up ready to march. Gilbert could see a line of horse-drawn carts were being loaded with boxes and provisions towards the rear of the train. Before long all the equipment, ammunition and food had been transferred to the carts and the train was signalled to move off south towards the main army base at Arras, leaving 240 men standing in formation on a rough road in the middle of the French countryside, the only sound being the distant booms of artillery and the incongruous melody of birds singing in nearby trees. A major gave the order to march and the platoon set off to join the 43rd Battalion of the 3rd Division of the Canadian Corps.

They marched for about two hours and arrived at a tented camp near the village of Neuville St Vaast. They were met by the commanding officer who welcomed them and told them that they were now joining a battalion that had achieved honours in battle and that he was confident that they would do likewise. The different sections were then allocated to tents that were pitched in rows across the field. The rain started soon afterwards and it became obvious that the tents were not fully waterproof. Gilbert and his chums were to have a cold and damp night.

They spent the next few days being issued with equipment, learning the names of their officers and familiarising themselves with how the camp was run. Some of the veteran soldiers told them tales of the battles that they had survived and described horrific stories of the effects of the shelling and poison gas. No doubt, soldiers had been winding up new recruits in this way since the first armies had fought.

It was only a few days after arriving that the whole battalion had to pack up, ready to move further north. Thankfully, Gilbert and his unit were able to load their kit bags onto wagons, but now they had rifles, helmets, ammunition and some food rations to carry instead. They marched through most of the day, which was thankfully dry, before arriving at another tented camp at the village of Bois des Alleux. The officers who inspected the camp were not at all happy with the way that it had been left by the previous battalion and they left muttering about writing negative reports to headquarters.

They stayed at the camp for four weeks, during which time they practiced shooting, bayonet attacks and, must usefully, were given lots of advice about how to negotiate 'no man's land' and avoid slipping into shell holes. They also learned some basic first aid and were shown how to use the emergency kits, with which they were issued. In between the training sessions, the officers organised boxing and wrestling matches between the platoons, as well as rugby matches. The weather remained unsettled and rain made the ground wet and muddy around the camp. Thankfully, their tents were more waterproof than the ones at the previous camp.

In the first two weeks of October the battalion were moved to closer to the Belgium border and Ypres. It became clear that they were being moved towards the front line and that it would be likely that they would soon be called into action. The mood of the soldiers became more thoughtful and sombre. On 18 October they were moved to the front line and relieved the 2nd ANZAC Battalion in their trenches to the west of the town Passchendaele, which was then behind the German front line. Gilbert found the trenches as bad as they had been described. The rain had left several centimetres of water in the bottom of the trench, so wooden duckboards were essential to be able to move at any speed along the trenches. These duckboards were both greasy and rotten, so it was easy to slip and find your foot in glutinous mud.

At various places along the trenches were sleeping shelters cut into the soil and rock. Trench humour named these shelters *hotel rooms*. Previous occupants had tried to make them dry and comfortable, but there was very little room for five soldiers and it was far removed from any sort of domestic or hotel room. The entrance was a rectangular hole about a metre wide and slightly more than a metre tall. Entering, therefore, involved stooping almost to a crawl. There was a lintel, about ten centimetres in diameter, made from the trunk of a small tree, supported by part of another tree on one side and half of a door post on the other. The roof consisted of a variety of timbers, some of which had scorch marks and had clearly been reused. Above the timbers was a sheet of rusty corrugated iron sheeting that held back the soil. The space itself was a wide rectangle cut into the subsoil and loose rock that made up the local geology. Ledges had been cut into the sides which provided four sitting and sleeping platforms on each side. The centre of the shelter was occupied by a crudely made wooden table, that also doubled as a sleeping bed for one of the soldiers. The floor of the shelter sloped towards the entrance, so that any water drained, and it was covered with dried bracken and reeds, that had clearly been collected from the marshland that was on the other side of the road that once ran through the area of their trenches.

Their kitbags were kept in a storage area further back from the front line, so they would not be able to change their clothes for many days, but this would be the least of their concerns. At least they would not be required to wear their kilts in the field. Early in the war Scottish regiments had been expected to go into battle in their kilts. However, the difficulties of keeping the kilts clean and free of lice was eventually recognised by senior staff and Scottish soldiers now wore khaki or in some cases tartan trews. The German soldiers nicknamed the kilted Scottish soldiers *the ladies from hell,* in acknowledgement of their fierce fighting prowess. The constant noise of shells and the frequent sniper fire reminded them of just how close they were to the German front line, while the persistent rain provided useful fresh water and also helped to wash the dirt from their clothes. On cold mornings, when the air was still, a cloud of water vapour would rise slowly from the damp soldiers' uniforms, giving a ghostly atmosphere within the trenches.

On 25 October the junior officers were called to the commanding officer's headquarters. Some seasoned soldiers watched them leave and then turned to Gilbert and his section who were sitting on the step that ran along inside of the trench wall.

'That's it then, laddies. The officers are getting their orders, it will be dawn tomorrow that we will be going over the top. Get your last letters written.'

Sure enough, when the officers returned they relayed orders to the sergeants, who then told the troops to clean their equipment and prepare for action. The platoon was positioned off a road that ran north-east to the town of Mosselmarkt, which was held by German forces. The objective for the attack was to push the German forces back and ultimately take the town of Passchendaele, to the east of Mosselmarkt. There was a shallow valley to the east of the road and behind the 43rd Battalion, through which a small river used to flow. Unfortunately, three years of bombing had blocked the usual flow of the river, so now the water had spread over a wide area creating a huge marsh. Gilbert and his section had had to carefully walk across wooden duckboards to reach the higher, slightly drier ground where they now lay huddled in their trench shelter. Gilbert shared the shelter with Jim Campbell, Andrew Hamilton, Harry McAuley and John Robertson. They had all been together since they met at Camp Hughes the previous year. They shared stories and cigarettes as they cleaned their rifles and checked their packs. Outside they heard the voice of an officer speaking to a shelter of men further down the trench, then a few minutes later a head appeared at their entrance.

'Good evening, men. I'm Lieutenant Shankland. I just thought that I would drop by and wish you good luck for tomorrow's push. We will be going over early, following an artillery barrage. You will need to follow your NCO and head for the ridge that you will see straight ahead. There will be many shell holes that will be full of water. Hopefully this rain will ease off so that you can run across the ground between the holes. Keep your heads down and try to zig-zag your way forwards.' Shankland paused as he studied the five men. 'Any of you lads born in Scotland?'

'Aye. I was born in Ayrshire,' Gilbert responded.

'Ayrshire! I'm an Ayrshire man myself.' Shankland replied excitedly. 'Where were you born?'

'In New Cumnock.'

'Were you a coal miner?' Shankland continued.

'No. A farmer.'

'Aye, well. I'm sure that you will show the Hun what happens when they mess with an Ayrshire farmer's lad. I'll see you on Bellevue ridge tomorrow morning.' Shankland's head then disappeared from view and the last of the evening light illuminated the inside of the shelter.

'Well, he sounded confident enough,' Harry commented.

'I didn't like what he said about the water-filled shell holes,' Jim responded. 'I heard a story from one of the veterans about a time when his section was making their way along duckboards across a marshy field, when they came across a chap who had slipped off the duckboard and was waist deep in mud. They tried to pull him out but he was stuck fast. They couldn't dig him out because the mud just flowed back in. After a while their sergeant told them to move on and he would send a message back to get the chap some help. Two days later when they came back along the same route the poor chap was still stuck in the mud, with only his head showing and completely mad.'

'Och, you dinnae want to believe the stories these guys tell ye. They just want to wind you up. I expect they have a big laugh afterwards, thinking that you believe them,' Harry replied.

The five men chatted well into the night, none feeling sleepy. However, they managed to doze in the early hours and had to be woken by their sergeant at five in the morning. The trench began to fill with men and short ladders were being fixed in place to allow the soldiers to climb over the top of the trench wall and start their attack. Gilbert could hear prayers being muttered and someone vomiting. Then the artillery barrage began to roll across no man's land, in order to clear away any German soldiers who may have crept into shell holes and also to try and shatter the barbed wire fences that lay in the path of the attack. The men listened as the shells could be heard landing further and further away from their trench. Gilbert could feel the ground shaking with each explosion. Then there was a silence and whistles blew. All the lead men climbed up the ladders and went over the top of the trench. Gilbert and his chums were soon also up the ladders and running along the muddy tracks between the shell holes, as the sharp reports of sniper fire, then machine gun fire erupted. Gilbert heard the bullets buzz through the air, reminding him of the midges that came up from the River Nith during summer days on Garclaugh Farm.

Gilbert and his section were making good progress towards the ridge when a shell exploded in front of them and a wave of mud rose above Gilbert. The advancing wall of mud seemed to Gilbert to be moving in slow motion, as he twisted away to shield himself from the impact of the soil and water. The wave of mud punched into his back and threw him onto the ground before burying him. Gilbert lay stunned by the impact of the noise of the explosion and the wave of soil that had buried him. He tried to move and push the soil off himself, but its weight was too great and he felt a pain in his back and leg. He started to panic, as his mouth was full of mud and he could not breath. He managed to get his arms under his chest and pushed hard to give himself some space in front of his face to try and spit out some of the soil. He was still struggling to breath and was contemplating his last moments when there was another explosion and he found himself flying through the air and landing on his back with such force that he spat out the mud from in his mouth and gasped in air. He was now lying on his back staring at the sky, his ears ringing and the sounds of gunfire seemingly a long distance away. Gradually his senses began to return and he tried to sit up, but the pain in his back and leg jolted him backwards. Eventually he managed to struggle up on his elbows and look around. Close by he could see the bodies of two soldiers. He realised with horror that these were Jim Campbell and Andrew Hamilton. He shouted to them but there was no response.

Gilbert lay on the ground for a long time, unable to move. It was clear that he had injured his back and could not stand. Even trying to crawl brought intense pain. A medic stopped to check on him at one time, but then moved on to treat other soldiers whose medical needs were more urgent. Gilbert felt very alone and his thoughts went back to his family and his sheltered life at Garclaugh Farm. Here he lay, surrounded by death, listening to explosions and machine guns that were busy killing more of the young men who had travelled with him from their peaceful lives in the Canadian prairies.

The rest of the battalion made progress in achieving its objective. There were several German pill boxes with machine guns that were put out of action by some brave soldiers. Lieutenant Shankland had managed to secure a base around one of these pill boxes and encouraged some of the advancing platoons to join him and push forwards. He acted as a rallying point and despite his own wounds led the attack to secure Bellevue Ridge for the 43rd Battalion. His brave actions led to the award of a Victoria Cross.

Canadian soldiers after the battle of Passchendaele

The retreat of the German forces allowed the medical units to collect the wounded, so by the end of the day Gilbert found himself on a stretcher being taken to a field hospital. He was patched up and taken to a hospital at Rouen where, along with many hundreds of other troops, his wounds were given more attention. Gilbert's physical injuries were relatively easy to treat, but the effect of being buried and losing all his colleagues from his section had damaged him in other ways. After a train and ship journey back to Britain he was admitted to Monyhill Hospital in Birmingham on 11 November, which was a hospital specialising in the treatment of shell-shocked patients. Fortunately, he only spent a couple of weeks there before being moved to Woodcote Convalescent Hospital at Epsom, in the southern suburbs of London.

Gilbert was able to slowly recover both physically and mentally from his war experience, which had only lasted six weeks. He wrote a letter to his mother explaining his situation.

Flora, of course, was keen to visit her son, so Tom arranged for his mother and himself to travel down to London to visit him at Epsom. It was a full day's train journey to Euston Station, where they spent the night at a local hotel, before travelling down to the hospital. Flora was very relieved to get out of the underground railway that they used for part of their journey, which frightened her, however, she was more relieved to see Gilbert. She had imagined that he might have some of the injuries that she had seen on wounded soldiers who had returned to New Cumnock with missing limbs or disfigured faces. Gilbert met his mother and brother Tom at the reception centre. He was dressed in the blue uniform that indicated that he was a convalescing soldier.

'We were so worried about you when we received the telegram telling us that you had been wounded. When I saw the telegram in the postie's hand my heart sank that it might have been worse news,' Flora told Gilbert. 'You've got injuries in yer back and leg you told me in your letter. Is it very painful?'

'It's no too bad, Mither. Just look around at some of these other men, they have far worse injuries than me. I can't complain. I am sure that the pains will go away eventually,' Gilbert replied.

Woodcote was a very large camp that had originally been set up for regular soldiers, but as more and more causalities started to arrive it was converted to a convalescent hospital. It could accommodate up to 3800 wounded and after the battle at Passchendaele they needed every one the beds.

'Have they told you how long they will stay here? Will they be sending you back to the front once you have recovered?' Flora continued.

'The doctors will look at me in a few weeks to decide whether I am fit enough to return to my unit. Not that there will be many men that I will know, I think most of my section were killed in the explosion that buried me,' Gilbert explained.

'You were buried?' Tom exclaimed.

'Aye. Yen shell buried me and then another yen blew me oot. I survived both, unlike my friends,' Gilbert explained.

'The guid Lord was looking after ye. He knew that you are a Godly man,' Flora told him.

They talked about his life in Canada, the journey over to Liverpool in the *Olympic* and other aspects of Gilbert's life that were new to Flora and Tom. Flora told Gilbert about John Todd courting his sister Chrissie and how she hoped that it might lead to a marriage. Then she brought up the subject of the future.

'When this war is over, why don't ye come back to Garclaugh? Andrew's health is not at all guid and he needs someone to help run the farm.'

Gilbert looked at his mother and then at Tom. 'I have to live through this war first, Mither. There is no sign that it is going to end any time soon. If you remember, everyone thought it would be ower by the first Christmas and here we are four years later, surrounded by broken bodies and with the cemeteries filling up with across France.'

'Aye. Yer right. Let's get you safely oot of France first, then we can talk aboot yer future plans.'

CHAPTER 11
1918

∞✿∞

Gilbert was to stay at Woodcote through Christmas and into the new year. He exchanged regular letters with his family and received visits from his brother John and his sister Chrissie, who accompanied their mother. On 7 January 1918 he was assessed by doctors as being medically unfit for active service. His thigh injury had left him with a limp and although he could walk, he suffered pains after a fairly short distance. After a brief stay back at Shorncliffe barracks he was to return to Canada on the *SS Olympic* on 23 February, via Halifax. Gilbert had to make a decision about his future and whether he would stay in Canada or return to Scotland.

All the Baird family had, of course, been kept up to date with Gilbert's progress and plans through their visits and the letters that he sent them. They were all glad that he had survived his dreadful experience at the front, although they all agreed that it had been a close-run episode. They had not yet heard if he would be discharged or would have to stay in the army, so were anxiously awaiting news.

***

John and Mary at Balladoyle were managing the farm through another cold winter that brought heavy snow in January. It brought yet more challenges to the young family. Mary was still bustling around in the dairy, even though she was now five months pregnant. She found it more awkward to sit on a stool and milk the cows by hand, so John had hired another dairy maid. She was only a young slip of a girl, as many of the older, more experienced girls had gone off to the munition's factory at Gretna for higher paid work, an annoying situation for which John was more than happy to share his opinion with anyone he met. He happened to be at the railway station delivering milk when he met with the manager, Duncan Wilson, from a neighbouring farm.

'Guid marning, Duncan. I hope that all is well with ye and yer family,' John boomed a greeting across the loading yard.

'Aye, Mr Baird. All's well. How is yer family?' Duncan replied.

'Aye, We're doing fine, despite the best efforts of the government to make life difficult for us farmers. What with taking oor best Clydesdales and young men, we now seem to losing the lassies to the munition's factory at Gretna. This war is going to drain the country of its work force,' John complained.

'I hear that Mrs Baird is expecting. Are ye planning on to breeding your own workers, as well as your cows and horses?' Duncan teased.

John laughed heartily. 'Well, my faither had five sons and twa daughters working on the farm at one time, so it's a Baird tradition that I am happy to continue.'

'I hope all goes well for the rest with Mrs Baird's confinement,' Duncan called, as he led his horse and cart down through the snow-covered lane.

John's eldest son, wee John, was ten years old now and, not so wee, was regularly working on the farm. He could harness up a horse, milk cows and even take a horse and cart out on the fields. His younger brother Jim also had a range of jobs that he was expected to do on the farm. This wasn't necessarily caused by a shortage of farm labour, but because their father wanted his sons to be hard workers, if they were to make their way in the world. To be fair to him, he set an example to his sons. Many of the neighbouring farmers commented on how many times they had seen him out digging ditches when the evening light was barely enough to see the spade. Some also commented disapprovingly on how the two young boys were also having to work long hours.

John's new wife, Mary, gave her two step-sons as much love and care as she could. She was aware of how much they had lost when their mother died and she did all she could to fill that void in the youngster's lives. She tried to keep in touch with the Stevenson family and arranged visits by Mungo Sloan and his wife, Jessie, who was Barbara's sister and the boys' aunt. Allan Stevenson now farmed Nether Cairn and had two boys himself, James and Allan, who were similar ages to John and Jim. Mary had suggested to John that it might be good for the two boys to stay with their cousins at Nether Cairn in the spring, while she was looking after the new baby. However, John was non-committal, because he realised that he would lose a couple of handy workers.

***

Springtime would bring a marriage to the Baird family, as well as a new baby. John Todd and Chrissie had had to arrange a marriage quite quickly and it took place on 27 May. To some they were an ill-matched pair. Chrissie was a loud-voiced woman who spoke her mind, like her father. John Todd was a much quieter and younger man who was happier to be in the background and make his presence felt in other ways. However, they say that opposites attract and that seems to have been the true in their case.

It also meant that another worker would be leaving Garclaugh and Andrew would have to find someone to help Mary in the dairy. He was still very much engaged in his cattle breeding and after the news of his world-record-breaking cow, May Mischief, had spread far and wide, there were no end of breeders clamouring to purchase a young bull or to lease of one of the established ones. It meant that Andrew did not need to worry too much about income for the farm and he could also hire help to look after his disabled brother, William, who was still physically fit and a large man. When they were all working out in the fields they sometimes took William outside with them, but had to tie him with a rope so that he would not crawl away and put himself into danger.

The war had stopped the export of cattle across to the United States, so the large cheques that he had received previously no longer arrived. The USA had remained neutral for much of the war, although they had supported European countries with loans and with raw materials. Their army was still small, but they had increased their merchant navy to meet the demands for goods in Europe. It was this increase in shipping to the Allied countries that had annoyed the German high command, who decided to take a calculated risk by warning the US government that their ships would be considered legitimate targets if they were taking goods to Britain and France. Public opinion in the USA was mixed and there were large communities of German immigrants who actively supported Germany. However, Germany was generally perceived as the aggressor and the news that many US ships and their crews were being sunk by U-boats brought the US into the war in 1917.

Army bases were set up around America when they introduced conscription, in order to increase the size of their army from 100,000 to 1,000,000. One of the largest of these new camps was Camp Funston in Kansas. There, 50,000 troops were trained there, prior to travelling over to France. In the early months of 1918, many residents in the neighbouring region of Haskell began to suffer with influenza and with the close connections with Camp Funston it was only a matter of weeks before the soldiers also started to suffer. In March 200,000 American troops were shipped over to France, some of whom would have been trained at Camp Funston. Inevitably the influenza was reported on some of the ships and in a relatively short time the influenza had taken hold amongst the troops across the battle front. Despite its rapid spread, the influenza, later called Spanish Flu, did not cause undue concern. Deaths from the flu were low and it was commonly dismissed as the 'three-day flu'. It caused problems amongst the population and the troops in Europe, but during the spring and summer of 1918 recovery was fairly quick.

***

Gilbert travelled back across the Atlantic on the *Olympic*, a much less crowded ship than the one that he had occupied the previous spring. He was heading for Halifax, but a very different Halifax to the one he left. On the 6 December, when Gilbert was still in Woodcote convalescing, a French cargo ship loaded with explosives collided with a Norwegian vessel in the straits next to the main dock area of Halifax harbour. The collision started a fire in barrels of benzol that were stored on the deck of the French ship, *SS Mont-Blanc*. Despite valiant efforts by nearby ships to extinguish the flames, although not by the crew of the *Mont-Blanc*, who abandoned the ship as soon as the fire broke out, its cargo exploded. The explosion is now considered to be the biggest manmade explosion prior to the atomic bomb that was detonated over Hiroshima. An area of over 160 hectares was destroyed by the blast, which was heard 200 kilometres away. Large factories and buildings on the harbour side were transformed to heaps of rubble and twisted steel. The workers in those factories, as well as on the dockside, were instantly killed, while only a handful of sailors on nearby ships survived.

Many people in offices and residential homes behind the dock area, who had been watching the fire from behind glass windows, were lacerated by the fragments of glass and left blinded. In all 2,000 people lost their lives, including the whole settlement of a First Nation tribe, whose homes were wiped out by the manmade tsunami that swept across the bay. The weather at that the time was bitterly cold, so the destruction of so many homes just added to the emergency and deaths.

When Gilbert arrived back on the *Olympic*, the buildings that he had walked past many months before no longer existed. A new docking area for the Olympic had been established further down the harbour, in a less damaged area. Since so many troops and equipment passed through Halifax, it was essential that some continuity was maintained. News of the disaster had been kept from the public and the troops in Europe, for fear of giving the Germans an opportunity for negative publicity, so the returning soldiers were quite shocked to see the devastation around the harbour.

Gilbert had to travel back to Winnipeg for a meeting with an army assessment team.

Following this assessment of his fitness for service, he was discharged from the Canadian army on 7 April 1918 as being medically unfit. He returned to McCauley and joined Hugh and Maggie at their farm. This gave him an opportunity to try and get his fitness back, as well as help on the farm with the chores that reminded him of his trouble-free youth at Garclaugh. For the moment, thoughts of returning to Scotland were pushed to the back of his mind.

***

Viruses have a habit of mutating as they spread. These mutations sometimes make the virus less virulent, but sometimes it can do the opposite. It would appear that the Spanish Influenza mutated towards the end of the summer months of 1918. Doctors began to report that their patients were suffering from pneumonia as a result of the influenza and that many more deaths were occurring. The virus had spread across the world, with even New Zealand reporting outbreaks. With the movement of troops across the world the spread was inevitable. Soldiers on leave from the front were keen to visit their families back in Britain, so brought back gifts from France, as well as the influenza.

John and Mary were oblivious to this potential threat, having celebrated the birth of their first son, Gilbert Edward, who arrived on 23 April. John was thrilled to have another son, while Mary was pleased just to have a healthy baby. John had decided not to send his two older sons to stay with their uncles at Nether Cairn, so John and Jim were able to welcome their half-brother into the family as well.

***

Over at Nether Cairn Farm, Allan Stevenson had taken his rifle out in the hope of killing a fox that had been become a real nuisance. During the early spring Allan had had some lambs taken by foxes and now one of them had decided that the chickens would make easier meals. Allan had gone out early, just after the cows had been brought in for milking, to search likely places for the fox's den. After a fruitless search he returned to the farmhouse, to be met by his dairyman who told him that he was having trouble with one of the cows. Allan dropped his coat and the rifle in the kitchen and went out to help his dairyman.

Allan's oldest son, Jim, had invited his friend Tom around to the farm that day and the two of them had been playing outside in the warm sunshine. Needless to say, their game involved re-enacting some of the war battles that they had read about in the newspapers. They had found suitable sticks to substitute for rifles and were acting out attacks on imaginary German pill boxes. After a while they came into the kitchen of the house to get a drink of water. Tom spotted the rifle that Jim's father had left propped behind the door and picked it up.

'Hey, Jim. Hands up or I'll shoot ye,' Tom called.

Jim turned to see Tom pointing the rifle at him. Tom's finger strayed to the trigger and there was a loud report, throwing Jim backwards against the stove and onto the floor. A bullet struck Jim in the head, killing him instantly. He was just twelve years old.

News of the tragedy spread quickly through the family and the neighbourhood. The lad Tom, of course, was distraught, as was Barbara's brother Allan, who blamed himself for leaving his rifle in the kitchen still loaded. The authorities decided to take no action, as the consequence of his mistake was punishment enough. The local paper reported the incident and it was hoped that other farmers would learn from the tragedy and take more prudent precautions with their own rifles. Allan, Williamina and their youngest son Allan were lost in their grief and the Stevenson family rallied around to support them.

CHAPTER 12
1919

꧁꧂

The entry of America into the war and the continued blockade of German ports eventually brought the end of the Great War, as it would later be called. At 11 o'clock on 11 November 1918 the war came to an end, to great rejoicing throughout Europe and beyond. However, it would be well into 1919 before soldiers started to return to their homes, as the army kept their troops in France and Belgium to help with the many problems, including, of course, dealing with the many thousands of corpses that were hurriedly buried in temporary cemeteries throughout the battlefield areas. Army discipline had to be maintained and so the conscripted young soldiers found themselves constrained by the same restrictions as when battles were being fought, however, now they were a victorious army. Food was still in short supply and when rumours started to spread through the army camps that food from Britain was being sold in local French towns dissent broke out that soon erupted in riots, especially in Calais. The officers attempted to arrest ringleaders, only to spark further and larger riots in other towns. A unit of newly recruited soldiers, who were brought in to quell one riot, ended up joining their disgruntled fellow squaddies. The mutiny eventually subsided when the army provided better food and upgraded the squalid accommodation that the soldiers were having to tolerate.

The soldiers in France had also had to suffer the influenza which had rapidly spread through the overcrowded camps. The Chinese labourers, who had been shipped over to France by the Allies and were treated little better than slaves by many British officers, had also been dying of the influenza, but without the same standard of medical treatment provided for the soldiers. This had also led to riots that were brutally suppressed using live ammunition. Gilbert may not have been aware of the troubles there taking place in France, but he was certainly fortunate to be away from it all.

As troops returned to their home countries, they took the influenza with them. It had now entered all European countries, as well as other countries around the world. It had, inevitably, reached both Cumberland and Ayrshire, and members of all the Baird families were struck down. At Balladoyle the flu rapidly spread, putting John, Mary, young Jim, the maids and the farmhands into their beds. Only young John escaped the initial infection, along with another youngster who had been taken on as a farm hand. These two boys ended up having to milk the cows, look after the horses, feed the livestock and take the milk to the station. It was a hard time for a few days until the adults recovered sufficiently to be able to take over.

At Garclaugh members of the Baird family also succumbed. Tragically, Mary later developed pneumonia and in early March she passed away, with Andrew at her bedside. As well as the grief of his sister dying and the concern over his mother, who at seventy-five was increasingly frail, he also had lost two family farmworkers within less than a year. He would be struggling to manage and was not a fit man himself. Once the family had recovered from the illnesses, a letter was sent across to Canada to encourage Gilbert to return home to help out.

***

During winter in Manitoba temperatures can drop down to minus 21° C and a metre of snow is a normal occurrence. By the time that Gilbert received Andrew's letter in March, the temperature had started to rise to minus 10° C. In the dry atmosphere of the Canadian prairies the powdery snow tends to blow around into drifts throughout the winter, so every morning there was a routine chore of clearing paths and doorways. Hugh and Maggie had had a baby girl the previous year, Gladys, so their family was now growing and farming had prospered during the war as foodstuff and horses were being bought by the army to be sent overseas. Hugh, Maggie, Gilbert and the children were sitting around the kitchen table enjoying the steaming porridge that would set them up to venture outside in order to sort out the animals. The postie had already called and delivered Andrew's letter and Gilbert was reading out the news from Garclaugh.

'Poor Mary died from influenza on 9 March. The whole family were infected but Mary seems to have suffered more than the rest of us. Her funeral was a few days later, to which many of our friends attended. Tom, Elizabeth and their oldest lad, John, attended. John is a fine young man now. Our John came up from Silloth, but his wife Mary had to stay with her bairn.

'Allan Stevenson attended, which was courteous of him as he did not know Mary well. I have not seen him since the funeral for his boy. From what I have heard Williamina is still struck with grief for her son. Such a tragedy.'

'Poor Mary. She was always rather sickly, mind. Must have been a shock to ma. That's the first of her bairns to pass on. We all thought that it would be William. This flu seems to be taking so many lives across the world. I hope that this is the last of the Bairds that succumb,' Hugh commented on the news in the letter.

Gilbert carried on reading various bits of news about neighbours and events in New Cumnock.

'With Mary passing on and Chrissie having left to be a wife and now a mother, we are very short handed at Garclaugh. I know that you planned to make a new life for yourself in Canada like Hugh, but I would ask if you would consider coming back to Garclaugh for a year or two until the soldiers return and we can take on more hired hands. Unfortunately, my health is not good and I can no longer do the sort of jobs that I used to be able to do. If you are willing to help us out and come back then I will pay for your passage back to Scotland.'

Gilbert paused and looked across at Hugh.

'Aye, well. I had a feeling that the letter might be going in that direction,' Hugh added. 'So, ye have a decision to make.'

Gilbert folded up the letter and put it on the table. 'Would you mind if I were to go back? Would it leave you short-handed as well?' Gilbert asked.

'Of course not, Gilbert. We would manage far better than Andrew by the sound of it. If you want to go back then here's yer chance, particularly if Andrew is going to pay for yer passage! You don't want to miss out on a free trip back to Scotland.' Hugh chuckled.

So, Gilbert packed up his few belongings and bade farewell to Hugh and Maggie and the children. He boarded the train back to the east coast and caught a ship to Liverpool.

***

Another Gilbert was making his own journey, although over a much shorter distance, across the kitchen at Balladoyle. John and Mary's son was now over a year old and had learned to walk. He had managed to take his first few steps to his half-brother Jim, who was holding his arms open to catch him.

'Well done, Gilbert' Jim told him as he carefully took Gilbert's hand to lower him gently onto his bottom. 'He looks very pleased with himself.'

'I am sure that you were, when you took your first steps, Jim,' Mary responded. 'It's a shame that yer faither did not see his first steps.'

'Well, I'm sure that Gilbert would be happy to take a few more steps when Pa comes in,' Jim replied, diplomatically.

It had been clear to Jim, since he himself was barely able to walk, that his father's first priority was the farm. He was a loving father and was clearly proud of his sons, but they would have to fit into the life of the farm.

John was not able to visit the farmhouse kitchen that morning as he had arranged a meeting with some of the other dairy farmers to discuss their cooperative, which was sending their milk by train across to Newcastle. This had been quite an innovative venture, as farmers were often at the mercy of buyers who could change their prices or reduce the quantity of milk that they accepted at short notice, leaving farmers to pour their milk down the drain.

As well as the milk cooperative venture, John was also keen to expand the size of the land that he farmed. He had already taken on the lease of a neighbouring farm to Balladoyle, called Pelutho Mire, but now he made enquiries about other farms that were for rent or sale. As well as his ambition to be a well-respected and successful farmer, like his father; another reason for his desire to expand was that Mary was expecting again, so there would be another mouth to feed and hope-fully another son.

***

Gilbert arrived at Liverpool on 30 March and was met by his brother John. They took the train up to New Cumnock, so John was able to hear more of the story of Gilbert's experience in the Canadian Expeditionary Force and at the battle of Passchendaele. John told Gilbert about the family news, especially about his new wife and his growing family. They discussed Andrew and his health problems. Gilbert had made the decision to stay at Garclaugh as long as he was needed and help Andrew run the farm.

Another piece of Baird news that John told Gilbert was that the old family farm at Sorn, South Blairkip, which had been farmed by their great grandfather since 1820, had now been rented by another farmer, John Templeton. John Templeton was married to their cousin Nettie, who had been born on the farm, so the Baird connection had not been totally lost.

Tenancies on farms were changing fairly regularly in these post-war times, as farmers who had lost sons in the Great War and had no one to inherit the tenancy decided to retire. Their elder brother, Tom, had taken on another tenancy of a farm on the Earl of Bute's estate at Dumfries House, called Glenside. His son, another John, who was only seventeen, now took over the running of Birnieknowe Farm, under his father's supervision.

In Cumberland, John, had identified a farm fairly close to Balladoyle that he felt could be a good purchase. It needed a lot of work to improve the land and make it productive, which would help in the negotiations for its purchase. John was not a man to shirk from hard work and he knew exactly what he would have to do, having already improved the productivity of Balladoyle and Pelutho Mire. The farm, called Flagstaff, was 200 acres and he managed to buy it for only £15 per acre. He would now be running three farms, making up a total of 450 acres.

In the kitchen at Balladoyle John was reading through the local news-paper to see the prices of farm produce that had been sold at the markets and Mary was having to step over his legs as she bustled around the kitchen.

'Why don't you read the newspaper in the parlour, John? Your legs are getting in the way where you are now.'

'What's that? Och aye. I've just about read all I want to read now. There are strikes taking place all around the country. The railway workers are threatening to go on strike, so that might affect the milk going o'er to Newcastle. So much for the *"land fit for heroes"* that Lloyd George proclaimed, it seems that we are descending into chaos. It's all these communist ideas coming over from Russia.'

'Well, these men who have been fighting for years have come back expecting to get jobs and look after their families. Now we don't need to make all the weapons and explosives, there's a lot of jobs been lost,' Mary replied.

John folded up the newspaper and placed it at the back of the kitchen table. 'Well, now that farming is becoming more mechanised there will be less men needed on the farms as well. There are likely to be a lot of unemployed soldiers looking for work for some years yet'.

The Great War was finally ended in June, when the Treaty of Versailles was signed. A victory parade was arranged and official celebrations took place. However, the mood of the returning soldiers and widows was not really celebratory. Following the parade many families focused their grief on the large wooden memorial that had been erected in Whitehall, inscribed with the words 'The Glorious Dead'. This temporary structure was later rebuilt in stone and became the Cenotaph.

Later in the year, it was decided that a less victorious and a proper remembrance event for the millions who died in the war was required. On 7th November an announcement from King George at Buckingham Palace was published in the newspapers.

Tuesday next, November 11, is the first anniversary of the Armistice which stayed the worldwide carnage of the four preceding years and marked the victory of Right and Freedom. I believe that my people in every part of the Empire fervently wish to perpetuate the memory of the Great Deliverance and of those who laid down their lives to achieve it. To afford an opportunity for the universal expression of this feeling it is my desire and hope that at that hour when the Armistice came into force, the

11th hour of the 11th day of the 11th month, there may be for the brief space of two minutes a complete suspension of all our normal activities. No elaborate organisation appears to be required. At a given signal, which can easily be arranged to suit the circumstances of the locality, I believe that we shall interrupt our business and pleasure, whatever it may be, and unite in this simple service of Silence and Remembrance.

At the appointed hour, just after the church bells and sirens had rang out, and much to the surprise of many people who believed that the two-minute silence would not be achieved, the country fell silent. Workers put down their tools, cars and lorries became stationary in the middle of roads, pedestrians came to a halt on pavements, horses were brought to a standstill, trains were stopped on the tracks. All movement stopped and a silence descended that had never been heard across British cities.

John and Mary were in Silloth at the appointed hour and both were moved by the emotional impact of the two-minute silence. They saw tears streaming from the eyes of men and women. As the two-minute silence came to an end, there seemed a reluctance and uneasiness to resume movement. Hats were replaced, throats cleared and gradually traffic began to move again. There were ghosts in many households and in every town and village, the ghosts of those who had fought and died for their country and who had been denied a burial and a homecoming. The Great Silence had aroused memories in those who were still managing their grief.

CHAPTER 13
1920

⟋∿⟍

Another healthy son, Robert Hugh, arrived at Balladoyle on 3 January. John was, of course, more than happy that the delivery was normal and that Mary remained healthy. He now had four sons, John, Jim, Gilbert and Robert, who would, no doubt, become farmers themselves and continue the Baird legacy.

Another new arrival at Balladoyle was a Fordson tractor. These tractors had been in use in the United States for some years and had now been exported over to Britain. Although John loved his Clydesdale horses and enjoyed breeding them, he was very aware of the shortage of manpower following the Great War. A tractor could do the work of a team of horses, with only one driver. Having taken on Flagstaff Farm, the shortage of manpower was even more acute. These early tractors did not have a three-point linkage for attaching implements; they would become the standard later for all tractors. However, they did have a cylindrical flywheel for running canvas belts that worked static machinery such as threshers and elevators. The Fordson tractor used petrol, although some tractors also used TVO, tractor vapourising oil. The arrival of the tractor caused some interest amongst the local farming community who took detours from the usual routes in order to try and spot the tractor working in the Balladoyle fields. However, perhaps the greatest interest, if not excitement, was shown by John and Jim, who were keen to drive it, or at least ride on it, themselves.

The tractor became very useful for helping to improve the land at Flagstaff Farm. Large steel wheels, with teeth around their rims, could be fitted to the tractor to give much more grip on the wet fields. It was then possible to use it to pull the loads of soil that was being brought up from new ditches. However, John used traditional horse and carts to fetch loads of pebbles form the beaches at Silloth, which were then put into the bottoms of the ditches to keep water flowing. Pebbles were also put into the gateways of fields to reduce the quagmires that were created when cattle were herded through. Overall, the drainage techniques that John learned from his father at Meikle Garclaugh, and that he was now applying to Flagstaff, would help improve the productivity of the farm. However, he also applied dressings of slag and kainit, a potassium-based traditional fertiliser that is especially good for grassland.

In September sad news came from Ayrshire when John heard that Barbara's sister Jessie had died, following a lung infection after an appendicitis operation. Her husband, his good friend Mungo Sloan, was, naturally, devastated. Just as her sister Barbara had done, she left behind two young boys. John and Mary travelled up to New Cumnock to attend the funeral. Without the availability of antibiotics, any operation brought the dangers of post-operative infections, however, with the Spanish Flu still within the community there was a strong possibility that Jessie's pneumonia may have resulted from the deadly influenza.

**

Andrew's health had deteriorated yet further since Gilbert had arrived at Garclaugh. It was almost as if Andrew had been hanging on until Gilbert arrived before he could stop fighting his condition. As a result of the failing battle with his pernicious anaemia, Andrew decided that he would sell off most of the herd of Ayrshire bulls and cows, which had spread the Garclaugh herd name around the world. Demand for Ayrshire cattle was still strong and there was always keen interest when Garclaugh bulls and cows were being sold at auctions. However, Gilbert was not interested in taking on the challenge of managing the herd, so there seemed to be little choice but to sell off the herd. It was not an easy decision, as he had worked with the herd, alongside his father, since he was a boy. He felt in some ways that he was ending his father's legacy as well as his own career.

A grand sale was arranged for 22 January at Garclaugh. Catalogues were distributed, which showed photographs of many of the Garclaugh herd, as well as some Birnieknowe and Mansfield Mains cows. It was a cold frosty day, but fortunately it kept dry. Gilbert cleaned a wagon and took it up to the station to collect farmers, cattle traders and visitors who had arrived by train. The sale was due to start at one o'clock, so Chrissie had come over to help organise luncheon for the visitors. The sale went briskly with top prices being paid, the average being £94 (which is equivalent to £4,600 in today's prices). Andrew did not feel well enough to attend the sale himself, although his main reason was that he did not want to watch the cattle that he had known since birth being sold. He came out later on in the afternoon when all that was left were a few local farmers, chatting by the remains of the food that had been set out on tables by the farmhouse, the other visitors having returned to the station. The remaining farmers, who included Andrew's brothers Tom and John, greeted him and told him of the success of the sale. They could understand Andrew's melancholy, as well as see the evidence of his illness in his gaunt face and frail frame.

Two days later, once all the auctioned cattle had been collected, the farm was a much quieter place. There were some beasts that had not been included in the big sale and a couple of cows that Gilbert had kept for milk in the house, but the byres still felt empty. Gilbert had started to plan what he would do with the farm, now that there would be no more dairy herd. He had decided to buy some fattening beef cattle for the meadows down by the River Nith and that he would get some fattening lambs for the top fields. He knew that there was a shepherd at Craigshiel, a farm on the Corsecon Hill only a short distance from Garclaugh, who had a large sheep flock, so he decided to take a walk up the lane to see if he would sell some lambs. Gilbert had also seen the shepherd's daughter, Mary, walking along the road that passed the drive to Garclaugh. He was also hoping that he might meet her when he visited.

Gilbert was successful in his visit to John Armstrong at Craigshiel. He managed to negotiate the purchase of some lambs and he also got to meet young Mary. Gilbert's war service with the Canadians was known within the community, so to Mary he was a war hero and she was quite taken by Gilbert's arrival and the time that he spent talking to her. He was clearly a shy and modest man, which she also liked. Gilbert's modesty regarding his war injuries were based on his knowledge that he was on the battle field for such a short time and that he had lost so many of his friends. Many families in New Cumnock and the surrounding district had had sons who did not return and others who were left with crippling injuries. Gilbert fully appreciated that he had been lucky to survive and to be only left with a limp and some back pain. Money was being raised within the community to commemorate the sacrifice of the 111 New Cumnock soldiers who did not return to their families with a memorial of some sort. This type of fundraising was being repeated in thousands of towns and villages throughout Britain.

***

Late May brought warmer weather and some sunshine. Andrew was sitting in a comfortable chair in the garden at the back of the farm house, with the view of the Nith valley and the Blackcraig Hill beyond. He had a blanket over his knees and was reading the local newspaper. Agnes the maid appeared from around the side of the house with a cup of tea and a bun on a tray.

'Mrs Baird thought that you might like a cup of tea, Mr Baird,' she explained.

'Aye. Thank ye, Agnes.' He made no movement to help Agnes, as he was becoming increasingly weak and did not want to drop anything. 'There will be some visitors coming over this afternoon to see me. If you would let me know when they arrive and you can help me into the dining room.

'Aye, I'll get the dining room ready for them. I'll just leave yer tea here on the table. Is there anything else that I can get for ye?' Agnes asked.

'No. That'll be grand.'

Agnes hovered around for a few moments then returned to the kitchen, where Flora had a list of jobs for her. Even though she was an elderly women Flora was still mistress of the household. Later in the day Andrew's doctor arrived, along with his solicitors, James Cunningham and Robert Dalglish. The last to arrive was Andrew's brother Thomas. Andrew was helped into the dining room where he prepared his final will and appointed Thomas, James and Robert as his executors. It was a sad legal event, as it was clear that Andrew had accepted that his end was close and that he wanted his affairs in order. He would be leaving his estate to his mother Flora.

Later that evening Agnes and Flora helped Andrew up the stairs to his bedroom and helped him get undressed and into his bed. The next morning, they found that he had passed away during the night.

Having gathered as a family for the sale of his Ayrshire herd in January, the family members gathered again to send Andrew on his way. His funeral was a large affair with representatives from many local and national farms, who recognised his many achievements. His international legacy as one of the top breeders of Ayrshire cattle would live on long after his death and would be a source of pride for the Baird family.

Later that year William, Flora's fifth son, would also pass away. He had lived much longer than anyone had expected and, in some ways, longer that some people had feared. His quality of life as a 37-year-old handicapped man was grim and it was a credit to the family that they had cared for him and had done what they could to improve his quality of life.

CHAPTER 14
1921

ᘓᘓᘓ

Manitoba is one of the prairie provinces of Canada and as such is subjected to hot, dry summers and cold, dry winters. However, during the summer in the south of Manitoba warm moist air comes up from the United States and meets the colder dry air from the north. This creates ideal conditions for tornadoes and in fact the southern parts of Manitoba are known as 'tornado alley'. Hugh and Maggie had witnessed some of these tornadoes from afar, but fortunately the tornadoes had all kept well away from Mansfield farm. In August, however, their fortune changed.

The day started like any other, but as the morning progressed dark clouds started to build in the south of McCauley. Hugh surveyed them with one of his workmen.

'It looks as if we might be in for a storm later today, Edward,' he commented. 'Perhaps we need to get things tied down in case it comes with a wind.'

'It certainly looks as if it is building and that black cloud is very threatening. Perhaps you need to tell your family to find somewhere safe to go?' Edward suggested.

'Aye. You might be right,' Hugh responded, rather distracted, as he stood staring at the clouds. 'We will need to make sure that the horses are all tethered well. We don't want them bolting and not seeing them again.'

Hugh went over to the farmhouse where Maggie was busy in the kitchen.

'We might be in for a storm in a while, there are some threatening clouds heading our way,' he told Maggie. 'Perhaps we should get the children settled down into a safe room?'

'What about Alex? He still upstairs in his bedroom after his tonsil operation yesterday,' Maggie asked.

'Well, his bedroom is at the back of the house, away from the storm, so he should be okay. Any winds won't blow directly onto the window. If the rest of you all get into the east parlour, then you should be away from any winds,' Hugh directed.

Hugh went outside again and looked in the direction of the clouds that were now even more threatening, and the black, swirling clouds seemed to be heading straight for the farm. Hugh and Edward started to tie down anything that they thought might blow away. The chickens were rounded up and put into their coop, although this involved much chasing, as the chickens were not used to being put into their coop in the middle of the day. By the time that they had secured as much as they could, the first tongue of a tornado had started to emerge from the swirling black clouds that darkened the sky.

'It's going to be a tornado,' Edward exclaimed, as he spotted the tongue of cloud stretching down to the ground.

'Well, we have done as much as we can. Let's get safe,' Hugh ordered. The two men walked briskly to the farmhouse to make sure that Maggie and the children were prepared. They did not seem to be in the house for very long before they felt the wind start to buffet the wooden walls. Hugh went upstairs to Alex's bedroom to make sure that all was well with him. As he opened the door to Alex's room the wind pushed and pulled on the window glass, until the glass shattered and showered Alex's bed with shards of glass. Then rain came horizontally through the shattered window frame spraying Hugh and Alex with water. Hugh grabbed Alex and carried him down the stairs to the east parlour where the rest of the family were lying on the floor. Little Gladys was whimpering and hanging onto her mother.

'Everyone, just stay still and the storm will blow around us for a little while then move away.' Hugh tried to be as reassuring as possible. However, the wind had got even stronger and he could hear the crashing of farm equipment being thrown around outside. A threshing separator was lifted up and thrown onto a grain box, crushing it, while the large barn was moved on its foundations. The raging wind ripped the roof off two barns and destroyed sheds, it picked up wagons and threw them across the yard. The cattle and horses in the barns were bawling with fear and desperately tugging out their halters trying to escape the 'beast' that was crashing in around them.

The family lay on the floor in the east parlour with the doors shut, as the wind continued to howl. Fortunately, no windows were broken in that room, although few windows survived in the rest of the house, but thankfully they remained safe. A swath of destruction lay across the McCauley district, with the remains of wooden buildings scattered across fields, along with dead chickens and other birds.

As the tornado moved away and the winds subsided Hugh and Edward went out onto the porch to survey the damage. Heavy wagons lay on their side some distance from where Hugh had left them. Sections of barn roofs hung precariously from beams and everywhere were small branches snapped from trees. They went to check on the horses which were stamping around in their stable stalls, their eyes wide with alarm as they pulled at their halters. Edward went into the stalls to calm them down and to make sure that there were no injuries. Thankfully all the horses seemed uninjured. The cattle in the fields had been able to run away from the tornado, so Hugh and Edward would round them up later.

It was a terrible loss and a frightening experience, but the family, like all the McCauley families who had been affected, picked themselves up, rebuilt and carried on.

***

Living with the possible destructive forces of nature is something all farmers accept, be it from tornadoes, floods or disease. The consequences of the Great War, however, had left deep and long-lasting scars in the hearts and minds of families across Canada, Britain and beyond. The global economy was in a poor state and many countries found themselves in a depression, with wages being cut and workers being made redundant. In the UK, the women who had been taking on the jobs of the men who were at the front suddenly found themselves out of work as their jobs were given to the returning soldiers. Women over the age of 30, who met certain property criteria, had been given the right to vote in 1918, however, during the war years many younger women believed that their work entitled them to equal voting rights to men. This injustice would simmer for several more years before being resolved.

Many of the soldiers who fought in the war came from British and French colonies. These soldiers wondered why they had fought to free countries in Europe, when their own countries were not free. The seeds of independence would begin to germinate in many colonies. Closer to Britain, Irish nationalism had erupted into violence, while across the North Sea the Russian Bolshevik army was busy invading eastern European countries in their campaign to create a greater communist nation. In Germany a little-known army corporal, called Adolf Hitler, would be elected Führer of a small political party called the National Socialist Party.

In New Cumnock the townsfolk gathered to officially commemorate the war memorial that had been erected with the names of all the 111 men from New Cumnock who had fallen in the Great War. It was a sombre occasion with many tears being shed, even though the war had ended three years previously. Widows, children who could barely remember their fathers and soldiers who had returned blinded or with missing limbs stood in silence as speeches were made and prayers were said. Gilbert, Flora and Gilbert's new wife, Mary Armstrong, attended. Gilbert and Mary had been married at the Dumfries Arms hotel in Cumnock. It was a quiet affair, with only close family attending to support the couple and wish them well on their marriage. The two newlyweds would live at Garclaugh with Flora, which Gilbert had now taken over as the tenant from Andrew.

Earlier in the year the last of the Garclaugh herd had been sold in a follow-up sale. Garclaugh Marksman, a bull that had an impressive pedigree, sold for an amazing 185 guineas (equivalent to £9,500 in 2021 prices). Flora and Gilbert both shared their disappointment that Andrew was no longer around to take pride in the esteem that his herd was held by the breeders of Ayrshire cattle. The money raised from the sale would help the family to purchase farms, rather than have to rent from landowners.

***

John was keen to return to Balladoyle after Gilbert's wedding, as he now had three farms to manage. His landlord Mr Kerr had been working with John on breeding Clydesdale horses and John was keen to breed some of his own show-winning horses. Mr Kerr was well known within the Clydesdale horse-breeding fraternity as one of the top breeders in the country. It was generally believed that the rich pastures of Cumberland helped to nurture the large, weighty horses that were so admired. Despite the arrival of a tractor in the fields it was still the horse that provided the most useful horse-power.

It was the dairy herd, however, that provided the income for the farms. The bulk of the cattle on Balladoyle and Flagstaff were descendants of Garclaugh bulls and cows and, as such, provided large quantities of rich milk that was in demand from the growing populations in surrounding towns. John, along with a group of neighbouring farmers, were sending their milk by train to a dairy in Newcastle. One morning his cooperative partner, Edward Anderson, met him at the station after they had loaded their churns of milk onto the milk train.

'Good morning, John. I hope that all is well with you,' Edward enquired.

'Aye. We are all well,' John answered. 'Ye look troubled. Is there a problem?'

'I hope not, John. It's just that we haven't received the payment for last month's milk,' Edward explained.

'How long is it overdue?'

'It is usually sent to the bank by the middle of the month, but we are now into the next month,' Edward answered.

'Have ye contacted the dairy? Perhaps it is an oversight,' John suggested.

'I tried ringing them their office, but the phone is not being answered. So, I sent a telegram last week, but have not yet had a reply.'

'I see. Perhaps we need to get over there and find out what is going on. The other farmers will be waiting for their milk cheques. Have any spoken to you?' John asked.

'I have had a couple ask me this morning, but I told them that we are chasing up the payments,' Edward replied.

'Well, we better get on chasing them, Edward. There's a train at ten-thirty this morning, let's get on over to Newcastle.'

So, the two men went home to change and then met again later that morning to travel to Newcastle. The journey took them close to two hours and they arrived at the dairy offices just before noon. However, the manager that they needed to see was nowhere to be found and the office staff told them that he had not been at his desk for some days. John and Edward searched the dairy for someone who could explain the lack of payment, but there did not seem to be any senior staff who could answer their questions. It was all very concerning. However, what was a greater concern was the large number of full churns that were being stacked in the yard without much activity to deal with them. It looked as if the milk production processes were coming to a halt. The two men were forced to return to Cumberland with the realisation that the dairy was about to close down and their contract was worthless. This bad situation would not affect just John and Edward, but also the other farmers who had been persuaded to join them in this venture.

Over the next few days their worst fears were realised, as the train company refused to accept their milk, as it was not being collected at the station in Newcastle. The consortium of farmers held a meeting in Silloth and angry words were aimed at John and Edward. John promised that he would reimburse the farmers for their lost income, a promise that he was to honour.

Mary spoke to John some weeks later, once the heat of the calamitous situation had cooled.

'How will we manage to cover our own losses, as well as pay back the other farmers?' she asked.

'Well, I made the money once before, I will just have to make it again,' John replied, before heading out to the dairy.

It was not long before John managed to negotiate another contract with a dairy in Carlisle. The milk that his sixty-five Ayrshire cows produced was of grade A standard and the herd was regularly inspected for evidence of tuberculosis. John and Mary supervised the milking themselves to ensure that everything was clean. Like his father had done many years previously, he even constructed a home-made sterilizer from an old boiler in order to steam clean each churn and all the equipment. Dairies were pleased to accept the milk from his farm, knowing that it was of such high quality. So, John did make the money again and was able to pay back the other farmers in the consortium for the money that they had lost. John's reputation as a fair and honest man was further enhanced within the community.

CHAPTER 15
1922–1928

❦

Following the upheaval of the Great War, political and economic changes caused further hardship to peoples around the world. In Eastern Europe the Union of Soviet Socialist Republics was established, while in Ireland the Irish Republican Army continued to fight for full independence, having rejected the Anglo-Irish Treaty that was signed the previous year. In Italy, Mussolini, of the Fascist Party, was appointed Prime Minister by King Emmanuel III, while in Germany inflation devalued the currency and caused hardship for ordinary people who, as in Britain, were trying to rebuild their lives after the war.

In Britain the economy started to settle and prices of foodstuffs and other necessities had fallen. People need to eat, so farmers had been able to rely on a steady income, even during the lean times. All the Baird sons were well established in their farms and prospects for them looked good. In February, all the sons, apart from Hugh in Canada, and Chrissie congregated at the kirk in New Cumnock for the funeral of their mother, Flora Mitchell, who passed away on 13 February 1922. Her health had been failing for some months and a particularly cold winter, with some of the worst snows for years, had been very hard on her. However, at the end she suffered a brain haemorrhage which brought a sudden end to her life. The kirk held a large congregation for the funeral, which befitted her status as a well-respected member of the kirk and the community. She was buried in the New Cumnock cemetery next to her husband John. The farmhouse at Meikle Garclaugh was even more empty now, with only Gilbert, his newly pregnant wife, Mary, and the maid, in residence. For Gilbert the house was still full of memories of the ten family members who once filled the house with laughter and loud conversation around a crowded dinner table.

Over in Cumberland John and Mary were on their way to crowding

Balladoyle with Baird offspring when they welcomed their first daughter, Flora Janet, to their family home. She was the first baby born after John's mother died, so it was fitting to name her Flora, whereas the usual Scottish custom would have been to name her after Mary's mother, Janet. However, they decided to use Janet as her second name. It was a few months later that Gilbert and Mary also announced the birth of their first child, John. The next Baird generation and the third John Baird had arrived at Meikle Garclaugh, just sixty years after the arrival of first John and Flora in 1866.

While the demand for milk and farm crops was maintained by a growing population after the war, the demand for coal diminished, which brought hardship in and around Ayrshire as mine owners cut wages in order to maintain their profits. The Labour Party was now no longer just a dream of Kier Hardie and his socialist peers; having come second to the Conservative Party in the general election, they then went on to form a minority government, along with the Liberal Party, under the leadership of Ramsay MacDonald. Kier Hardie had become unpopular at the outbreak of the Great War by encouraging workers to refuse to fight in a capitalist venture and he died in 1915 while trying to organise a pacifist general strike. The support for the Labour Party had undoubtedly been increased by the actions of the mine owners and other employers who sought to maintain their profits at the expense of the workers. The seeds of future widespread discontent were being sown.

***

In Cumberland, John and his two elder sons were working hard to improve their farms. Wee John, who was sixteen years old, was by now an experienced farmer. His father had put him into manage a new farm that he had taken on, called Wampool, while his younger brother Jim, who was only fourteen, was put in charge of Flagstaff Farm. Not only did John expect his two sons to cope with the demands of running a farm, he expected them to reach high standards. The quality of milk was being regularly tested by the dairies and certificates were issued to acclaim A grade milk, for which they received 3d per gallon extra, making their milk income up to 1s 2d per gallon. (This would equate to £1.70 in today's prices. The average price paid to dairy farmers today, for a gallon of milk, is £1.22.)

National
Milk Publicity Council

This Certificate is
awarded to

Messr. John & James Baird

for Proficiency in the Production
of Clean Milk

MILK
FOR
HEALTH

Signed _A.B. Allan_

Date _July 25th 1926_

Despite the discovery that tuberculosis could originate from infected cows that passed on the tuberculosis bacteria through their milk, the spread of the disease was still a problem and large quantities of milk could easily become contaminated from one infected cow within a herd. In 1922 the Milk and Dairies Act was passed which outlawed the sale of milk from infected cows. Suspected infected cows could be tested using a procedure which involved injecting the cows with an inactivated mix of proteins from the tuberculosis bacteria. There would be an immune response from any infected cow that would reveal itself as a lump on the cow's skin, so indicating that the cow had tuberculosis antibodies and hence was infected. The pasteurisation of milk was also becoming more widespread, which would kill tuberculosis bacteria, as well as other contagious bacteria, however, it would be some years before pasteurisation became widespread and mandatory.

As well as ensuring that the reputation of Baird milk was maintained, there was also a continuing requirement to improve the drainage on the low-lying fields. Wampool Farm, in particular, was only a few metres above sea level and at high tides sea water would back up along the River Wampool that flowed through the farm. Keeping ditches clear and creating new drains was a constant task on the farm. The ditches were dug by hand and it was back-breaking work. However, the work that wee John put into draining the soil, paid dividends with increased crop yields and better quality grass for the cattle.

The year 1925 proved to be a hot and dry summer, so the grass that had been set aside for hay had not grown as thick as would be needed to ensure a good supply for the winter. However, the men were busy in the fields at Balladoyle, with their sharpened scythes cutting the long grass while the sun was shining. Wet grass would make mouldy hay that was unhealthy for the cattle, as well as the men who handled it. Sweeping the long razor-sharp blades to cut the grass close to the ground was quite a skill and the men who were hired in by John prided themselves on how much they could cut in a day. As he was on his way to bring in the milking cows John took a detour over to the hayfield to see how the work was progressing. He took wee Robert with him, who was happy to get away from the house and into the fields. He loved running and as his father was talking with one of the men, Robert raced across the field towards one of the workmen who he recognised.

'Hello Billy!' he shouted as he grabbed hold of Billy's arm and swung himself around Billy's body. As his leg swung around Billy, the back of his lower leg slid down the sharp blade of the scythe, which sliced through his skin and his Achilles' tendon. Billy, taken unawares of wee Robert's arrival, let go of the handle of the scythe and looked down at the young lad, who was now screaming with pain at his feet. Everything had happened so quickly that he did not realise that Robert was injured.

'What's up, Robert?' He asked as he bent down to comfort the boy. It was then that he saw the blood and the wound that was producing it. He looked around for someone to help him and saw that John was now walking briskly towards them both. The other men had stopped working and although most stared over in puzzlement at the noise, a couple who were nearer realised that something that needed urgency was taking place. In a very short time, a small crowd had gathered around the bleeding boy.

'I didn't see him, Mr Baird. He just swung around my arm and his leg must have gone down the blade,' Billy pleaded.

'Don't blame yerself, Billy. The lad should have had more sense,' John assured Billy. 'I will run back to the farm and drive the car to the bottom of the lane. If two of you would carry him, I will meet you down there.'

John raced back to the farm house to tell Mary and to get car started to take Robert down to the doctor's surgery. Naturally Mary was distraught to hear what had happened and grabbed some clean clothes before joining John in the car. They soon met up with brothers Billy and John Steward, who were waiting by the roadside, and Robert was carefully lifted onto his mother's lap in the rear of the car. She wrapped a cotton cloth around his leg to stem the flow of blood and cuddled him tight to comfort him.

Fortunately, the doctor was at the surgery so Robert was rushed into his examination room. The doctor examined Robert's cut leg.

'It's a clean wound but his tendon has been cut. I can sew it up but it will be tricky getting his tendon reconnected,' the doctor announced, over the top of Robert's screams. 'We will need to get him strapped onto the table, hold him down while I get some bandages to tie his leg.'

The doctor carefully located the ends of Robert's Achilles' tendon and tied them together using gold wire that would not corrode or cause any infection once his wound had been sewn up. He could not use any anaesthetic on such a small lad, so while he carried out his delicate task Robert squirmed and squealed under the firm grip of his father and mother. Eventually his wound was sewn up and his leg bandaged to keep it clean and to prevent Robert moving his leg while it healed. He was carried home and put to bed, where he stayed for a few days. Remarkably, after a few weeks he was walking again and made a full recovery, with no evidence in his gait of his previous injury. The story of how wee Robert kicked a hole in the plastered wall with his good leg, while having his tendon sewn up in his other leg, was often told by the staff at the doctor's surgery.

***

John and Mary were strong believers and attended St Andrews United Reformed Church in Silloth, and in 1924 John was ordained as an elder into the church. He and his family were to remain closely connected with this church and over the years John helped to raise money for building projects and donated considerable sums himself. They were able to bring their second daughter to the church in early 1925 to be baptised Mary Kathleen.

Wee Mary, as their new daughter would be called for many years, much to her annoyance, struggled to digest cow's milk when her mother tried to wean her. They needed to solve this problem, as Mary could no longer feed her baby herself. The doctor, surprisingly, suggested feeding the baby with turnip juice. So, each day Mary, helped by the maids, chopped up turnips and squeezed the juice into a feeding bottle. This tedious task went on for many months, but it was successful and wee Mary drank the turnip juice and put on weight. Mary, as well as the maids, were glad when her baby eventually grew out of her allergy to cow's milk and moved onto the solid foods.

In 1926, Gilbert and Mary at Meikle Garclaugh were thankful that their second child, Agnes, although she would be called Nancy, did not have the same problems with cow's milk. As well as celebrating the birth of his daughter, Gilbert had the opportunity to recall a dangerous situation that had taken place when his brother Hugh fell from a hay cart onto the train track that ran through the fields at Meikle Garclaugh. A similar escape took place on the same railway crossing when a young lad was leading a horse and cart of hay from the bottom meadows and he failed to notice an approaching train. The passing engine missed the eleven-year-old James Paton, but grazed the nose of the horse. This incident highlighted the dangers associated with having a railway running through a farm, as Jim was to find out at Flagstaff Farm.

By the mid-1920s the situation in the British coalfields and in other industrial areas had become desperate for the workers. Mine owners had reduced wages yet again and this led to a national strike. This was not the 'land for fit heroes' that Prime Minister David Lloyd George had extolled at the end of the war, as a task for the government to achieve.

John and Mary at Balladoyle were absorbing the news of the strike, which they had read about in the newspapers, but they had also heard a broadcast on their newly acquired wireless radio. As well as the coal miners going out on strike, the newspaper print workers downed tools, so the only news outlet was through the radio, which greatly increased its popularity. Jim at Flagstaff was particularly intrigued by this new form of entertainment and visited Balladoyle more frequently in order listen to the music that was being broadcast through the wireless. He was keen to get one installed at Flagstaff, but his father told him, in no uncertain terms, that it would be too expensive.

Flagstaff was now becoming much more productive as the new drainage and fertilisers were improving the soil and, consequently, the crops. Jim, at only sixteen years of age, had now been managing the farm for his father for two years and had acquired agricultural knowledge and skills. As well as the dairy herd Jim was keen to breed Clydesdale horses, having developed a real passion for horses. Mr Kerr, who still owned Balladoyle, and a long member of the Clydesdale Horse Society, was happy to advise Jim and suggest suitable Clydesdale stallions from neighbouring farms.

CHAPTER 16
1928–1932

᠙ᡇᢅᢙᡇᢆᠯ

In 1928, Hugh and Maggie in Canada decided to sell their farm, Mansfield, and move to Rocanville, where Maggie set up a popular boarding house and Hugh became a weed inspector. This was only thirty-five kilometres from McCauley, but it was over the province border from Manitoba, in Saskatchewan. Hugh had become tired of farming, particularly as it was no longer bringing in the same income as before and during the war, and wanted a change. Maggie was happy to set up her new business, although she was sad to leave the home that they had set up together in McCauley.

As Hugh was visiting farms in his role as weed inspector, he became interested in the Bear Creek–Tantallon area, where he noticed a number of springs which produced flows of crystal-clear water. The local farmers told him that these springs never stopped flowing, even during periods of drought. Perhaps they reminded Hugh of the Blubber Well that sprung from the ground at Meikle Garclaugh. This is also a spring that flows constantly throughout the seasons and Hugh would have been very aware of the well, as he would have had to fetch water from it on many occasions. When Hugh was a boy all the water on the farm would have had to have been brought from wells. Hugh promoted the idea of bringing water from these 'ever-flowing' springs into the village of Tantallon. His idea was met with enthusiasm and he was asked to be the 'foreman' of the project. The project proved to be a great success and homes and local businesses were soon getting with fresh, clean water from their taps. Hugh received the gratitude of all the local residents.

As well as Hugh making a name for himself in Canada, John was now well established in Cumberland as a prominent and successful farmer. He was expanding his influence and had decided to purchase a farm called Polshill, across the river from Meikle Garclaugh, that had come onto the market. Conscious of the need to make provision for his daughters, as well as his sons, the farm was purchased in the names of

Flora and Mary. He then asked John Todd and his sister Chrissie to lease the farm as tenants, which they were happy to do. So, John had now increased his stock of farms to five. In the meantime, he was still busy at Balladoyle helping the dairy maids with the milking.

'So, Mr Baird, when are you going to get one of these new mechanical milking machines and put us out of work?' Janet, one of the dairy maids, asked John, when he visited the byre to see how the milking was progressing.

'And why would I want to spend a good load of money buying a machine, when you lassies are doing such a grand job?' John replied with a chuckle. 'I've had a look at these machines and I would still need maids to wash the teats, attach the machine and then take it all off when it has finished. Dinnae fret, the machines won't be putting you oot of work for a lang time yet, Janet.'

'That's good to know, Mr Baird, I've never understood how anyone can think that a machine can replace my delicate hands,' Janet replied, to the amusement of the other maids.

John gave a good laugh at Janet's saucy cheek as he left the byre to inspect some of the calves in their pens. A dairy herd did not just consist of the cows that were being milked. There were younger heifers that would need to be raised and brought into milk and there were breeding bulls that had to be selected in order to improve the quality of the calves being born to the milk cows. It was the selection of good breeding bulls and cows that had created the famous Garclaugh herd, a herd now spread around many farms following his brother Andrew's death and the subsequent sale of the herd.

As John walked around the farm checking on his livestock his thoughts turned to the new farm machinery that was becoming available. Perhaps he should look into the new airline milking apparatus that he knew was being installed in other farms. If it increased the speed at which the cows could be milked then perhaps he could increase the size of the herd and the amount of milk he could produce.

As he left one of the calf sheds, he was nearly knocked down by a boy who was running very fast.

'Watch oot, laddie,' he shouted to the fleeing figure.

'Sorry, Pa,' Wee Robert shouted back over his shoulder.

'That laddie's leg certainly shows no effects of being sliced through with a scythe,' John muttered to himself, as Robert's brother Gilbert also came running past him, clearly chasing Robert.

'You'll hae to run faster than that to catch him, Gilbert,' John laughed, watching his two younger sons disappearing around the corner of the byre. They were growing up fast and would soon be able to help out more around the farm.

Meanwhile, John's eldest son, wee John, had been courting a local girl, Agnes Ritson, from Parkhead Farm at Causeway. In April 1931 they married and their first child, Jessie Stevenson, was born in the September. While over at Flagstaff, Jim's eye had also been taken by Bella Dixon, who worked as one of the dairy maids.

***

Over at New Cumnock John's brother Gilbert had decided to give up the tenancy of Garclaugh and take on the tenancy of Glenside, which had previously been farmed by his eldest brother Tom. Tom's health had not been good, so he had decided to retire from farming. So, not only had Garclaugh seen the last of its famous Ayrshire cattle, but now the Baird family were leaving as well. Gilbert wanted to be able to manage a larger farm, that did not have half its acreage under water every winter, as well as a farm that did not pose a threat to boys and horses bringing carts over the railway tracks. Glenside was part of the marquess of Bute's estate; its walled gardens bordered onto the farm boundary, although the marquess rarely visited his estate at Ochiltree.

Just after Hogmanay 1932, two officials from the local health authority arrived at Glenside Farm. They were checking on local children, as there had been an outbreak of diphtheria locally. Gilbert and Mary invited them into the parlour and young John and his sister Agnes were brought in to be examined. The children had not been well over Christmas and both had coughs. After the examination by the doctor the officials spoke to Gilbert and Mary.

'I'm afraid that it looks as if your children have contracted diphtheria. We will need, therefore, to isolate them at a ward at the hospital at Cumnock,' one of the officials announced. 'If you can pack a bag for them, then we can take them over now.'

Gilbert and Mary stood in shocked silence as they absorbed the news that they had just been given, before Mary spoke. 'But it's just a cold, they just got a wee cough.'

'That may be the case, Mrs Baird, but we will need to check. If they have got diphtheria, we don't want them spreading it to other children at school,' the official replied. 'We do have the authority to take them, without your permission.'

Mary reluctantly went upstairs to pack some clothes for John and Agnes, while Gilbert explained to the children what was happening.

'John, you will hae to mind yer sister whilst you are at the hospital. We will come to visit ye this evening,' Gilbert told his son. 'When you get better you will be able to come home.' Agnes, only just five years old, began to cry.

The children were put into the back of the car with their small suitcase and Gilbert and Mary watched as it drove down the drive and disappeared down the road to Cumnock.

When Gilbert and Mary visited their children that evening the children complained that they had been given injections. Agnes told her mother that she wanted to come home and hung around her neck. The nurses were very vague about what injections the children had been given and told Gilbert and Mary that they would be able to speak to the doctor the next day. They returned to a quiet Glenside and sat in the parlour with worried expressions.

Diphtheria is a bacterial infection that mainly affects the throat, but can also affect other organs. The symptoms can be mild or severe, but are usually characterised by a barking, croup cough.

The next day they returned to Holmhead Hospital in Cumnock. As they waited for the start of the visiting time, one of the doctor's approached them.

'Mr and Mrs Baird?' the doctor asked.

'Aye,' Gilbert replied.

'I'm afraid that your laddie, John, has not been at all well today and he has a fever as well as a very swollen throat. We are treating him for diphtheria. Your daughter also has a fever, although her symptoms are not as severe.'

'You gave them injections yesterday,' Gilbert stated, waiting for an explanation.

'Aye, we gave them a dose of anti-toxin to counteract the effects of the bacteria. Most children respond well after they have had an injection. How well they respond depends on how long they have had the infection.'

'Can we see them now?' Mary asked, when she noticed that the visiting time had started.

'Your son is in the intensive care ward at the moment and we can let you see him from a distance, but you will not be able to speak to him.'

Mary's tears ran down her face as she saw her son John lying in the hospital bed with his swollen neck. Agnes was more active and again hugged her mother's neck. It was an emotional time for both the parents and their children. Gilbert and Mary returned to Glenside and prayed for their bairns. However, when they returned to the hospital the next day, they were told the devasting news that John had died during the night and that Agnes was now in the intensive care ward. Agnes died the next day.

Various members of the family rallied around to support Gilbert and Mary in their shock and grief. Their life together had seemed so happy, having recently taken on Glenside Farm and their two children, apparently so healthy. John and Mary travelled up from Balladoyle for the funeral, at which the two children were buried side by side in the kirk at Cumnock.

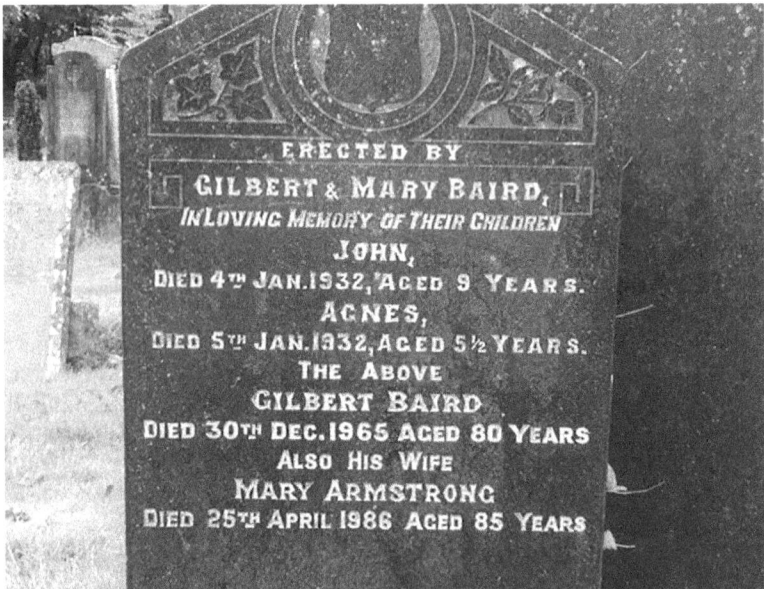

On their return to Balladoyle Mary gave her own children big hugs and John made arrangements for them all to be vaccinated against diphtheria.

John had decided to lease another farm on the edge of town, called Silloth House Farm. It was owned by a Mr Todd. The farmhouse was bigger and it was generally had better land for both grass and crops. The family moved from Balladoyle to live at the new farm. John was not only interested in improving his family's situation but also decided to invest in an airline milking machine in a new byre that had recently been built at the farm. His son Gilbert was now fourteen years old and had left school, so John had him working on the newly leased farm, learning farming skills.

Robert, in the meantime, was still at Causeway Head School, where he and his friends got into mischief and did their best to avoid the head-master, Mr Childs, who they called Daddy Childs. During breaktimes Daddy Childs patrolled the school grounds with his leather strap and used it on any child who he spotted breaking the rules. Robert and his friends decided to remove stones from a wall that bordered the play-ground, so that they had an escape route if they saw Daddy Childs on patrol. The hole that they created was big enough for them to crawl through and disappear from his searching gaze. Unfortunately, as the hole was expanded, the wall above it eventually gave way and a section collapsed, fortunately there were no children beneath the stones.

Robert was, in fact, a bright boy and performed well in his studies. He was head boy in his last year at school. His teacher approached John on one occasion and asked what Robert would do when he left school.

'Why, he will come to work on the farm,' John replied.

'Robert is a bright boy. He's too clever to just work on the farm,' the teacher replied.

John was furious at this statement and responded. 'You're another one that thinks that farmers are stupid.'

Clearly the teacher had no knowledge of how John had progressed from a farm manager to running six farms and had used his brains to become a wealthy man. So wealthy that he was able to provide St Andrews United Reformed Church with a number of interest-free loans. One loan was to acquire a manse for the minister, while another was to help build a church hall. In later years John also helped the church acquire a second-hand pipe organ. These actions were typical of John, who was keen to support the community, both religious and secular. His eldest son, John, continued his father's commitment to the church by becoming an elder himself in later years.

John's second son, Jim, continued his improvement work at Flagstaff Farm. The dairy herd was flourishing, as was his breeding of horses. As well as the Clydesdale that he bred for farm work and for shows, he also acquired a horse that was more suitable for pulling a gig and for riding. He loved riding this horse around the farm and had thought about entering it for horse races. As well as a passion for horses he had also developed a passion for the dairy maid called Isabella Dixon, or Bella, as she preferred to be called. Their intimacy grew and inevitably led to Bella telling Jim that she was pregnant. Jim was shocked, but told Bella that they would get married. This was not a plan that impressed Jim's father.

'What! There is no way that you are going to marry that dairy maid,' John told Jim, after Jim had informed him of the news of Bella's pregnancy and their intention to get married. 'You will marry into a good family, with proper connections.'

Jim argued with his father, but John was adamant.

'I will give her some money so that she can support the child, but she must not have any contact with you again or seek any further support money,' John announced.

And so it was, that John gave £360 (£25,000 in today's money) to Bella and made her sign a document stating that she would not seek any further money from the Baird family. She left the farm and on 22 March 1932, gave birth to a boy, who she named James Baird Dixon. Bella then left the infant with her mother, for her to raise, and obtained work as a dairy maid at another local farm. Jim, however, felt guilty about the manner in which Bella had been treated and when he visited Cockermouth, where Bella's mother lived, for the hiring fair, he would call at the house to visit his son. Jim's illegitimate son grew up calling his grandmother 'mother', and only met his real mother occasionally when she called at the house. He eventually joined his mother when he was five years old, after she married a local man, Harry Bowers.

CHAPTER 17
1933–1936

❧⌇❧

As dairy farms expanded in the 1930s, farmers were finding it more and more difficult to sell their milk at a good price. Milk processing dairies could cancel contracts or reduce the price that they were paying famers and because milk was a perishable commodity, farmers found their incomes being squeezed, as John and the other farmers who had joined a cooperative to sell milk to the dairy in Newcastle had found this out to their cost, and certainly John's cost. The National Farmers Union, therefore, established a national cooperative called the Milk Marketing Board (MMB). Farmers could sell their milk to the MMB and the dairies were forced to buy milk from the MMB. The large majority of dairy farmers joined the MMB scheme, as they now had had a guaranteed buyer for their milk and a set price. The MMB scheme came into fruition in 1933. The MMB was also able to set hygiene requirements and supported action to reduce TB in cattle, so that the consumers of the milk also benefitted. The days when housewives bought milk that was labelled from a churn in a farmer's cart were fast disappearing. Milk was now supplied in sealed bottles with cardboard lids.

Now that the dairy unit at Silloth House Farm was up and working with the newly installed airline milking machines, John decided that trying to manage a herd at Balladoyle farm as well stretched his time and his workers to their limit. He decided, therefore, to give up his leases on Balladoyle and Pelutho Mire Farms and concentrate his efforts on Silloth House Farm and the other two farms.

Over at Wampool Farm John and Nan were settled and the land was starting to show the benefits from all the hard work that had been applied to drain the fields and boost their fertility. Crop yields had increased and the fields produced plenty of quality grass for the dairy herd. Little Jessie was now over two years old and was a joy to them both. Nan was in the kitchen preparing food for their Christmas meals, which was just over a week away. She knew that John would be coming in for his mid-morning cup of tea, so she had boiled the kettle on the stove and when she heard John come in through the back door she filled the teapot and poured two cups of tea on the table. She turned around to find the milk jug as Jessie chattered away, playing with one of her dollies.

'Do you want some tea, Dolly?' she asked her doll. Jessie then made her way over to the table and reached up towards one of the teacups, holding the hot tea, taking hold of the handle.

Nan was busy filling a jug with milk when she heard a scream and turned around to find Jessie on the floor with the teacup broken beside her. The front of Jessie's dress was steaming with the scalding tea that had spilt over herself. John had also heard the scream and ran into the kitchen. Nan filled a jug with cold water and poured it over the distraught infant. Little Jessie was screaming with pain and the skin on her chest had started to blister. Nan desperately tried to remove her dress, which still contained hot tea. As the dress came off Jessie, the extent of her scald became more evident.

John rushed out to get the car started, in order to take Jessie to the local hospital. They had wrapped Jessie in a blanket, as she was now shivering from shock, and Nan held her on her lap and they travelled as fast as they dared. The doctors at the hospital treated Jessie as best they could. Her chest was now blistered with a severe burn. The hospital decided to keep her in overnight and John and Nan visited her the next day. They watched her riding on a toy bike from a balcony, since the doctor had told them they wanted to keep her in for another day and they were concerned that if Jessie saw her parents, then she would get more distressed, wanting to come away with them when they left. However, she seemed to be recovering, so they went home encouraged that their little Jessie would be home with them soon.

A severe scald or burn damages the skin and creates an entry point for infection. In a time before readily available antibiotics there was little that could be done to halt the spread of infection, once it had entered the body. If it reaches the blood stream then the invading bacteria can sweep around the body causing multiple organ failure.

Tragically, this is what happened to Jessie. Less than a day after the visit by John and Nan, Jessie died from septicaemia.

The farmhouse was now deathly silent, without the noise of a lively toddler. The family rallied around to give support to John and Nan, but there was little that could be said or done to relieve the grief and sadness of losing a child. Nan blamed herself for not keep a closer watch on Jessie when she was in the kitchen. She wished she could have taken Jessie home with her when they saw her riding the little bike in the hospital. She would carry that guilt all her life.

***

As the 1930s progressed the Baird family in Cumberland prospered, with Silloth House Farm being the centre of their farming enterprise. This was despite a collapse in economies and employment across Britain and other countries. All three farms were producing milk that was being sold to the new Milk Marketing Board. Compulsory tuberculosis testing had been introduced for dairy herds and infected animals were culled, with compensation being paid to farmers. Along with vaccinations, this led to a considerable reduction in the incidence of tuberculosis within the population.

Despite his teachers encouraging Robert to continue his academic studies, he had left school now and was working on the farm, learning the knowledge and skills of farming. His sisters, Flora and Mary, were having to catch a train from Silloth to Carlisle to their secondary school each morning, but at the weekends they found time go out and about on the farm. On one wintry occasion they were walking across the frozen fields back to the farmhouse when they decided to try and cross a frozen ditch. Mary decided to try and walk across the ice that stretched across the surface of the water, but it was not as thick as she thought and she fell through into the icy water in the ditch. Fortunately, Flora was close by and managed to grab her and help her out of the water. The two sisters made their way back to the farmhouse and Mary crept in as quietly as possible to change her clothes, in order to avoid her mother, who would have given her such a scolding.

In 1934 John and Nan had a baby son, called John, who brought back joy and noise into the Wampool farmhouse. Three years later, Mary, their daughter arrived, closely followed by Gilbert the next year.

Jim at Flagstaff had continued his particular interest in horses with a breeding programme for Clydesdales, that were still in use on the farm despite the arrival of tractors and other machinery. Jim had been working with other local Clydesdale horse breeders and as a result had bred a fine stallion that he named Baird. The stallion was entered into various shows, where it won many accolades. It was with some pride that he was able to collect the winning rosettes and prize money at the Royal Highland Show and at the Royal Agricultural Show.

Later that year Jim was made an offer for the horse by a breeder in Canada, at a price that was too good to turn down. So, Jim's champion Clydesdale horse Baird travelled across the Atlantic to Canada, where it became the overall champion at Toronto Winter Fair and was admired and received further accolades and prizes. Back in Cumberland, Jim also pursued his personal breeding desires by marrying Margaret Wilkinson in the spring of 1936.

Wee John at Wampool had taken an interest in the local hound trail sport, which matched hounds against each other over a long man-laid scented course. Originally set up to test fox hounds, it had become very popular with ordinary country folk on either side of the border, but particularly in Cumberland. The hounds were trained to follow a scented trail, knowing that there would be a special treat of food waiting for them when they finished. The hound owners would wait in a field by the finish line, staring across the slopes of the hills trying to spot their hound that they hoped would be leading, as there were money prizes for the fastest hounds. As the hounds started to appear the owners would shout and bang the food dishes to encourage their hounds. The shouting increased with many of the spectators, who had put betting money on their favourites, joining in with the hound owners. Breeding fast trail hounds was within the budgets of ordinary folk and was taken as seriously as the breeding of the Clydesdales and Ayrshire cattle, with significant sums of money being paid for breed bitches and stud dogs.

***

At Silloth House Farm John was relaxing in his chair reading through the newspaper. Breakfast was finished and Mary and the maid were busy clearing away the dishes. John was making various grunting noises as he read news in the paper that interests him.

'Aye, and what's happening in the world today?' Mary asked.

'Well, this business with the king wanting to marry this divorced woman seems to be occupying most of the politicians doon in Westminster. They don't want the woman to be queen,' John responded from behind the large broadsheet paper.

'So, do you think he will give up this woman?' Mary asked.

'Well, if he wants to be crowned king then he may have to give her up. She is married to an American and was married before him as well. Hardly going to be a very respectable queen,' John replied. 'Talking about queens, I see that the *Queen Mary* liner has gone on its maiden voyage to America. Perhaps we could take a journey oorselves yen day and go across to see Hugh and his family?'

John pushed the newspaper onto his lap and looked across at Mary. 'There's talk of another war, would ye believe. Ye wud have thought that the world had had enough of war. We've only just finished putting up memorials to the Great War and here they are complaining aboot the way that Hitler and his nasties are running Germany. They want to keep the Germans under control.'

Mary changed the subject to more local issues. 'Flora is complaining about her teeth again, John. Perhaps you could run her over to the dentist to have a look at them. They certainly look very inflamed and there's quite a bit of blood when she brushes them.'

'Aye. Well, I have to go oer to Wampool later, so I could call in on the way. Perhaps she should get them all taken oot and get false yens like mine.' He chuckled at his remark.

'For goodness sake, John, she only fourteen. She doesn't want false teeth at her age,' Mary responded.

John looked suitably chastened. 'Well, I'll see what the dentist has to say. I'm sure he will be able to suggest what she can do to sort them oot.'

***

In October a large group of unemployed men took it upon themselves to march from Jarrow, in the north of England, down to the Houses of Parliament in London. This was a peaceful protest to highlight the unemployment situation, which had improved in many areas of Britain, but was still as a high as 20% in the north-east. The marchers were supported during the long march with food and water from local people that they passed on the way. The Trades Union Congress and the Labour Party distanced themselves from the marchers, who they viewed as being communist led. Politicians at Westminster also refused to meet with their representatives for the same reason.

In March 1936 German soldiers marched into the Rhineland, a region of Germany that had been declared a demilitarised zone after the Great War. The Allied governments dithered about what to do about this clear breach of the Treaty of Versailles that the German government had signed in 1919. After various statements of disapproval, they chose to do nothing.

Later that summer Germany hosted the Olympic Games and the National Socialist government, headed by Adolf Hitler, used the occasion to flaunt the superiority of its organisations, its infrastructure and its athletes. The Nazi games, as they would later be called, and the unbridled nationalistic and racist atmosphere that surrounded them, sowed concerns in the minds of leaders of other European countries. Some politicians worried that a new war was looming and tried to persuade the government to make preparations. Some of these warnings were heeded and preparations were made that would have dramatic consequences for John at Silloth House Farm.

CHAPTER 18
1937–1940

◦⌒◇⌒◦

$\mathbf{A}$s Easter approached in 1938 John picked up a lung infection and was confined to bed with pneumonia. His sons Gilbert and Robert were now experienced and knowledgeable about the farm's business and John knew that his daily presence around the farm was not needed, so he resigned himself to stay in his sick bed.

Gilbert was cleaning out the milking parlour when he heard a vehicle drive into the farm yard. He looked out of the parlour door to see two men in suits, one carrying a briefcase, climbing out of the black car. The two men started to walk towards to farm house.

'Can I help you gentlemen?' Gilbert shouted across the yard. The two men stopped and turned to look at Gilbert as he walked towards them.

'Mr Baird?' enquired one of the men.

'Aye. Mr Gilbert Baird.'

'We were looking for Mr John Baird, the farmer.'

'Mr John Baird is ill in bed at the moment. I'm his son, how can I help?'

'We are from the Air Ministry. We need to inform you of a decision that has been made regarding this farm. We have already spoken to Mr Todd, the owner, but now need to speak to Mr Baird,' the first man continued.

'Well, as I explained my father is not well enough to leave his bed, so you will have to speak with me,' Gilbert responded. 'Let's go into the house.' Gilbert then led them over to the farm house.

Gilbert told his mother, Mary, the significance of the visitors and they all sat around the dining table while papers were removed from the brief case that had been opened on the table. The senior of the two Air Ministry men spoke.

'The Air Ministry have chosen this farm and some of the surrounding area as the site of a new airfield that is going to be constructed. Therefore, you will have to vacate the farm. You will, of course, be compensated for the loss of your tenancy and livelihood whilst you locate to another farm, if you choose to do so.' The ministry man paused to allow the news to be properly absorbed. There was a long silence before Gilbert responded.

'So, when do you want us to vacate the farm?' Gilbert was thinking that this would take many months to arrange another tenancy or buy a farm.

'We will take over the farm on the first of April. We will start by putting up some buildings that we be a base for machinery required to construct the runways and hangars.'

'Is this an April Fool's joke?' Gilbert retorted.

'I'm afraid not, Mr Baird. We will want to start construction work in a few weeks' time,' the more senior of the two men replied.

'A few weeks! We can't vacate the farm in a few weeks. Where are we supposed to go? We have a pedigree dairy herd, what are we supposed to do with all the cows?'

'We appreciate that there will be difficulties, so a generous compensation grant will be made available to help you with a move to a new farm. We can arrange the compensation quite quickly.'

'Can we appeal against this decision?' Gilbert asked.

'I'm afraid not. This decision has been made at a high level and with the threat of another war, this airfield will be important for the defence of Britain.'

Gilbert and his mother looked at each with resignation. Mary broke the silence. 'I had better break the news to your father.' She pushed her chair back from the table and the two ministry men stood up as she left to find her way up the stairs to the bedroom, where John had heard the discussion going on downstairs and was wondering what it was about. Gilbert waited for the loud reaction from his father.

'So, how do we go about getting compensation?' Gilbert asked the two men. The second ministry man, who had remained silent up to that point, delved into his brief case and withdrew some official papers.

'Your father will need to sign these documents. We would advise that he consults with a solicitor to make sure that you, or rather your father, who is named in the tenancy contract, fully understands what needs to be signed. If you need any further explanation then you may ring me at this phone number.' He passed over his business card to Gilbert. Gilbert read the name and the details, passing to look upwards as he heard his father's raised voice from the bedroom upstairs. He knew that his father would not be a happy man.

'I am sure that you and your father will have further questions about how the exact details of the construction of the airfield. Perhaps we could call next week to collect the signed papers and to answer the questions that you may have,' the senior man explained.

The official briefcase was repacked and closed, then both men from the Air Ministry stood up to leave. Gilbert showed them to the door and watched them as they returned to their car. His mother appeared at his shoulder.

'Well, I was not expecting that sort of news when I woke up this morning. Your father wants to speak with you.'

Gilbert was correct, his father was not a happy man. Gilbert tried to repeat word for word what the ministry men had told him. John tried to express his anger, but ended up in a coughing fit. Eventually he calmed down and was able to pass on his instructions to Gilbert.

'Call oer to Mr Todd and find oot what he has been told. I cannae believe that they want us oot of the farm in twa weeks. Leave those papers behind, I will have a read through them.' He flopped back onto his pillow.

Later Gilbert returned from his visit to Mr Todd and went upstairs to the bedroom.

'Well Mr Todd has received the same news. He has been offered a very generous compensation for giving up the farm, so he's a happy man,' Gilbert told his father. 'He seems to think that we will get good compensation as well, especially with all the improvements that we have done around the farm. The tenancy compensation scheme will also guarantee that.'

'That may be, but where are we going to find a suitable farm in such a short time? What are we going to do with the herd? We need to get the ministry to delay the construction work for a couple of months, whilst we sort things oot,' John replied.

'They said they would call around next week to collect the signed papers. Do you want me to take them around to the solicitors?'

'Aye. Get George Wilson to study them and let us ken if they are all in order. See if you can get him to call in after the weekend. I should be feeling strong enough to come doonstairs by then.'

Work carried on around the farm while its fate and that of the animals were being discussed. The cows still needed to be grazed and milked. Robert had been out ploughing when the ministry men called, so was told the news when he came in for his lunch. He didn't see the point in finishing the ploughing if the field was going to be turned into a huge building site in a matter of weeks. Robert was more concerned about his pending dentist appointment, when he was going to have all his teeth removed. He had developed a gum infection that would not shift and it was now affecting his teeth, a number having become loose and two falling out. His fourteen-year-old sister, Flora, had also developed the infection and the doctors had proposed the same drastic solution. Dentists were quite proud of the false teeth that were now available and regularly offered folk the removal of the whole set of their troublesome teeth. The prospect of removing the source of painful toothache must have outweighed the prospect of having to use false teeth for the rest of one's life.

Meanwhile Britain celebrated the coronation of King George VI, after his brother David had abdicated the throne rather than give up marrying Wallace Simpson. Britain also had a new prime minister, after Neville Chamberlain took over from Stanley Baldwin. One of Neville Chamberlain's first tasks was to try and restrain the expansionist ambitions of Adolf Hitler. Despite his apparent success in persuading Hitler not to reclaim more German speaking territories, there was a general mood that war was imminent. This view was reinforced when gasmasks were issued to the population in 1938. At Silloth House Farm the preparations for the defence of Britain were more tangible as construction machinery arrived at the farm and bulldozers grubbed up hedges into large heaps that were then set alight, causing large clouds of smoke to drift over the Solway Firth. Crowds of onlookers came out from Silloth to watch the construction work. The Baird family could only watch in dismay as the improvements that they had made to the farm were destroyed.

John had failed to persuade the Air Ministry to delay construction of the airfield, however, when he was told the size of the compensation that he would receive he realised that it might be possible to purchase another farm outright. He now had two sons who could help him to set up a new farm somewhere else. He searched the property section of the national newspapers and sent out enquiries for available farms. He eventually selected a few possible farms, however, in early 1938 he set out with his daughter, wee Mary, and his brother-in-law Edward Bell, for the Scottish border town of Kelso, where there was to be an auction for a farm not far from the town, which he had visited and believed would suit their requirements.

The auction was due to take place in Kelso itself, so Mary decided to wander around the town and visit some of the shops, while her father and uncle were at the auction. After a while she returned to the corn exchange, where the auction was taking place, and stood by the steps that led down from the main door. It was not long before various men appeared at the door and made their way down the steps passing Mary. Mary could hear them in conversation. One of the men was saying to another, 'Fancy paying that price for the farm,' while another man in a small group was saying, 'He'll never be able to make enough money to pay back that sort of price.' Various others groups of famers left the corn exchange muttering similar views. After a time, her father and uncle Edward emerged from the doorway. They were followed by another farmer who turned to him and said, 'How do you expect to get your money out of the farm paying that sort of price?'

John responded, somewhat indignantly, in his recognisable booming voice, 'I don't want to get my money out of the farm, I want to keep it in!'

Wee Mary realised that her father was the person that the various men had been talking about. She was now worried that her father had paid too much for the farm. He had in fact paid the princely sum of £12,000 or £20 per acre (equivalent to £830,000 or £1400 per acre in 2021) for Harpertoun Farm. Despite the slightly above-average price paid, John was well pleased with his purchase.

The move to Kelso, nearly 90 miles from Silloth, would not be an easy undertaking. It would require a whole train to be hired in order to transport the animals, machinery and household goods. John paused at the bottom of the steps contemplating all the arrangements that he would be required to take. He turned to look at Mary.

'Come on then, wee Mary. Let's get hame and tell yer mither that we have got a new farm.' Mary followed her father over to the car that was parked in the centre of the large square that dominate the centre of Kelso. As she walked to the car, she glanced around at the buildings and shops that would soon be her new local town.

***

The next few weeks were a frantic time for everyone. The preparations for moving the contents of Silloth House Farm were helped by the generous compensation from the Air Ministry, that provided extra funds to cover the cost of the move to Kelso. Mary, helped by Flora and wee Mary, had to supervise the packing of all the household contents into tea chests, while Gilbert and Robert packed tools and important pieces of farm machinery into crates. While in the fields large excavating equipment was busy digging the foundations that the aircraft hangers and other buildings required on the airfield. When all the machines stopped in the evenings, the cows would graze around the piles of earth and the deep holes. Miraculously no cows fell into the unfenced pits that had been dug into the meadows. In the fields that Robert had been ploughing, when they first heard about the requisition of the farm, bulldozers scraped off the topsoil and flattened the land ready for the concrete that would be poured to lay out the runways.

Over at Wampool John and Nan welcomed the birth of their son Gilbert, who followed on just a year after their daughter Mary was born. While at Flagstaff Jim and Maggie had kept pace with John and Nan by producing a daughter Margaret, who had arrived soon after their son, yet another wee John, born the previous year. Both John and Jim would have mixed feelings about their father and half-siblings moving across to the other side of the country. Although they might welcome the opportunity to be able to manage their farms without their father overseeing their decisions, they also realised that they would not have their father's advice and experience when difficult decisions needed to be made quickly. However, both John and Jim had been learning the craft of farming from an early age and had already proved themselves as competent farmers.

***

The day of the big move eventually arrived. Arrangements for a train had been completed and the station at Silloth had been prepared with extra pens to hold the cattle, prior to being loaded onto trucks. Gilbert and Robert had already taken quite a number of the bits of machinery over to the station in the week before and they had been loaded onto the wagons that were held in sidings. The residents in Silloth were quite surprised to see a herd of cows walking past their front gates and some mothers took their children out to watch the spectacle. John had called in favours from local farmers to borrow workers to help with the large operation. Thankfully by midday every cow, horse, sheep, chicken, dog and piece of farming machinery had been loaded and secured. John and Gilbert would drive the car and the farm van truck over to Kelso, while the rest of the family had to settle down amongst boxes of personal belongings in a carriage at the front of the train, waiting for the station master's whistle and the gentle shunting of the trucks as the engine set off for Carlisle and its onward journey to Kelso.

John had made arrangements at their new farm, Harpertoun, for the arrival of the dairy herd. The old byre was cleaned out and various pens were added to make more area suitable for the number of cattle arriving. Two of the men working at Silloth House Farm, Billy and John Stewart, had agreed to travel over during the previous week in order to carry out the preparation work. So, when the train finally arrived at Kelso station, John felt that he had done as much as he could, in the short time available, to prepare Harpertoun for its new owners.

The train station was situated on the southern side of the river Tweed, that bisected the town of Kelso. This meant that the animals would have to be herded along the main road to the old town, across the Tweed bridge, through the town centre and then on a long journey north to Harpertoun. It would be a long walk for cattle not used to such a journey. It would also bring new challenges in getting the cattle safely through the town centre, with its open square, to the narrower roads beyond, along which it would be easier to drive the herd and lead the accompanying horses. Gilbert and Robert supervised the unloading of the cattle into temporary pens that had been erected. Eventually all was ready for the great trek over the river and through the town. All went reasonably smoothly, with one amusing incident when one of the town's residents complained to Gilbert and asked what he was going to do about the many droppings that were being left on the town streets.

'Oh, we won't want them, you are most welcome to help yourself,' he replied with a wry smile and a twinkle of his eye. The resident was not impressed by Gilbert's reply.

As well as preparations being made at Harpertoun, preparations for war had started around Britain, with gas masks being issued to the population. Constructions for a possible war now started to involve the whole country, not just a farm by the Solway estuary in Cumberland. By that time the house at Silloth House Farm had been demolished; a newcomer would find it difficult to imagine that a farm once existed under the large concrete hangars and runways at the new airfield. Where cattle and tractors provided the most noise that one could hear; soon aeroplanes would drone across the sky above Silloth.

View of Silloth with the airport and the site of Silloth House Farm.

***

On the 1 September 1939 German forces invaded Poland, forcing Britain and its allies to declare war. Twice in John Baird's lifetime Britain's young men would be dragged into conflict. In October all men between the ages of twenty and twenty-three were required to register with the military. Both Gilbert at twenty-one and Robert at nineteen turned up at the local military office in Kelso to register. As both were working within a protected profession, they avoided enlistment, however they both agreed to join the local Kelso Home Guard.

Following the consternation caused by the declaration of war, there was a flurry of national action, including the evacuation of children from the cities into the countryside, in anticipation of German bombing raids. Children from Glasgow and Edinburgh arrived at Harpertoun, Wampool and Flagstaff, as the farming families 'did their bit' to host children. However, after a several weeks and then months of war inactivity, some parents came to collect their children and took them back to their urban homes. Many of the children returned home with stories about how they had been made to drink milk that came from cows, not bottles, and how eggs came from chicken's bottoms, not cardboard boxes. However, at other farms the children stayed for most of the war years and they became part of the family. It was not unusual for children, whose parents were killed during bombing raids, to be adopted by the farming families that had hosted them throughout the war years.

Although some people called the lack of military action in Europe the 'phoney war', there was plenty of action taking place in the Atlantic as the German U-boats targeted merchant ships bringing food and other supplies into British ports. The decrease of vital resources coming into Britain brought about petrol rationing and later food rationing. There was now even more urgency to ensure that farms increased their production to replace the lack of imported foods. The government introduced a National Farm Survey of all agricultural land over five acres. Farms were rated as A, B, C or D according to how well they were being managed. If it was considered that a farm was not being managed properly and therefore not providing sufficient crops, then an advisor would be appointed, often a farmer from a neighbouring well-managed farm.

Although John had purchased Harpertoun, mainly with compensation money from the loss of his tenancy of Silloth House Farm, he had still had to borrow additional money, up to the limits that the banks would provide. These additional funds were barely enough and he had been forced to borrow some money from relatives in order to cover day-to-day running costs. The dairy had been completed, so he was at least able to get milk production underway properly and get a regular income into the farm. Gilbert took over the management of the dairy herd, while Robert concentrated more on the arable side of the farm, getting fields ploughed and crops sown. During the war years, food production was a top priority, so there was no problem finding customers for the farm's produce.

Machinery was now commonplace around farms. Many farms had acquired a tractor and most had some type of static engine that helped to work all sorts of chopping, crushing and lifting devices. The early tractors could do little more than move a wagon or pull an implement through the soil. The static engines worked a flywheel from which belts could be attached. These belts would transmit the rotation of the flywheel to the machinery that was needed to be operated. A tractor also had a small flywheel to which long belts could attached to run threshing machines, elevators and mills. The belts could be many metres long and they spun at a considerable speed through the air. Some of the machinery that was becoming increasingly common on farms was inherently unsafe and most of the workers on a farm treated the spinning wheels and shafts with respect, however, familiarity can breed a lack of care. Many farm workers broke bones, lost fingers and even limbs when that care was forgotten.

At Harpertoun a large barn stood behind the new byre, which would be needed to be filled with hay for winter fodder. Trailer-loads of loose hay would be brought up to one side of the barn ready to be unloaded and moved to one of the bays at the far end. This task would once have been done manually by many workers armed with pitchforks. At Harpertoun a hay lift system had been installed consisting of a four-prong grab that could be lowered onto the trailer to collect a load of loose hay. A long rope then lifted the grab-full of hay upwards and along a rail to the far end of the barn, where the grab could be opened and the hay dropped into the correct place. The consistency and precision required for this system to work still relied on a horse to pull the main rope, rather than a static engine. One summer's day John was helping out in the barn by supervising the grab at the trailer, ensuring that the four prongs closed properly onto a load of hay. On one occasion the grab closed the prongs and John shouted for the horse to be led forwards. However, as the grab lifted John saw that the prongs were not fully engaged so he shouted for the horse to be stopped and he leaned forward to pull on the offending prong. Unfortunately, the man leading the horse did not hear John's shout and the horse continued to pull on the rope, which was now lifting John off the ground. John struggled to get his hand out from behind the prong, as he was being lifted further and further into the air. By the time that he had released himself he was now twenty feet off the ground, onto which he found himself falling. His landing was hard and painful. He shouted in pain. He had broken his leg.

John was taken off to the local hospital where his leg was reset and plastered. John's mobility was now quite restricted, but it did not stop him from sitting on the back of a corn binder during the harvesting of a field of barley a couple of weeks later, with his plastered leg propped into a position so that he could still work the binder.

While John was working with a broken leg under the July sunshine, young pilots battled with German bombers over the fields in southern England. The Battle of Britain had commenced, as Hitler tried to force Britain to negotiate a settlement with his government. However, Winston Churchill had taken over as prime minister and had success-fully overseen the evacuation of Britain's expeditionary forces from the beaches around Dunkirk in the previous month. He made it plain to Hitler and the British people that surrendering was not going to be an option.

CHAPTER 19
1941–1946

☙❦❧

Although there had been huge progress in reducing diseases that affected both people and animals, antibiotics were still not commonplace. The vaccination programme against tuberculosis, tetanus and diphtheria had helped to reduce the number of deaths, particularly amongst children. Dairy cows were now being routinely tested for tuberculosis. Herds could attain a certificate through the Attested Herd Scheme to show the cleanliness of their milk and all the Baird dairy herds, both in Cumberland and in Scotland, had received such certificates.

Unfortunately, some diseases would appear without warning or apparent cause. In 1941 there was an outbreak of foot and mouth disease in Ireland, just across the sea from Cumberland. The disease managed to jump across to the UK mainland and infected herds in Cheshire and Cumberland. This wasn't the only disease issue that concerned Jim at Flagstaff one morning.

'I was speaking to Pat Wilson this morning,' Jim told Maggie. 'He was telling me that one of the doctors in Silloth is telling people that the dysentery outbreak in town is caused by infected milk. Pat was worried that people would stop buying his milk. I'm wondering the same.'

'What makes this doctor think that the dysentery has come from the milk? I thought that dysentery usually comes from bad water,' Maggie replied.

'I would like to know why this doctor thinks it has come from the milk. With the restrictions to the movement of cattle from the foot and mouth outbreak, it's the last thing we need. I'm getting fed up of just one problem after another,' Jim complained.

'We have certificates showing that our milk is clean. How can this doctor blame our milk?' Maggie responded.

'I'm don't think he is blaming just our milk, but people will still think that all the milk from local farms is to blame. We will need to try and put a stop to this. I wonder if we can get the Milk Marketing Board to put out a statement in the newspapers about the cleanliness certificates?'

'It's worth a try. They are supposed to be supporting dairy farmers after all.'

The situation became worse when the local doctor was quoted in the local Silloth newspaper as suspecting that the dysentery was associated with infected milk and later Jim found out that the doctor had warned some of his patients about using milk from the Flagstaff herd. Needless to say, Jim was livid, but there was little that he could do. He could not prove that his milk had not been the source of the dysentery, since people would just say that he had now cleaned up his milk processing. The sale of his milk to local customers dropped as a result of the slanderous accusations.

Another source of long-standing irritation for Jim was the railway line that ran through the middle of the fields at Flagstaff. The armaments testing site at Silloth was now a busy place, as were the docks. Trains ran more frequently along the line, making it difficult to move the cows to pastures on the other side of the tracks to the dairy. Jim had visited Harpertoun and had seen the fertile land that was present in the area. It was certainly an improvement on the flat and often waterlogged soil that surrounded Silloth. Jim wondered whether a move to a farm in Kelso might be advantageous. In the meantime, he took pleasure in the arrival of his daughter Flora, followed the year later by another daughter, Mary.

***

The young men on the Baird farms were fortunate not to be called up for the war. They were needed on the farms to help with the production of food. Their cousin Alex, out in Canada, had been signed up to the army and was now part of the Canadian Expeditionary Force. While Gilbert and Robert were now full members in the local Home Guard. A couple of Robert's friends had also joined him in the Home Guard, but after a rather excessive session at the local pub they rolled up to the local recruiting office and found themselves signed up to the regular army. Fortunately, Robert had more sense and wished them well, as they left on the train that took them to their training base. Gilbert and Robert reported for training twice a week with the Home Guard, where they were taught how to fire a rifle, with the two proper rifles that their unit that had been issued. Their uniforms took quite a while to arrive, but eventually they were all kitted out with rifles that had been manufactured for the First World War and with ill-fitting uniforms. Their sergeant, a veteran from the First World War, drilled them until he was satisfied that they were up to his exacting standards.

Their first call to real action happened one evening, following a report that a suspected German parachutist had been spotted coming down in fields near Kelso. Their Home Guard unit were called out to search the fields in order to apprehend the suspected German spy. The unit were split into pairs and they spent many hours on a cold and dark night tramping through wet fields on a fruitless search for a parachute. Eventually Robert and his partner decided that it must have been a swan that had been seen and conscious that they would have to be working the next morning on the farm, decided to crawl under a milk churn stand outside a local farm, in order to find a quiet and dry spot to sleep. Imagine their surprise when they found that the space below the stand was already occupied by their sergeant!

While the British population had to learn to prepare meals from rationed ingredients, particularly meat, farmers and their workers could supplement their rations with produce from the farms. Inspections did take place by local government officials to ensure that as much of the farms' produce as was required was being sold officially. Sugar was in particular short supply, however, some farms had bee hives that required sugar to keep the bees alive over winter. So, these farms received an extra ration of sugar for the bees. Needless to say, some of the sugar ended up in cakes and desserts on the dinner table.

As the war continued all farms started to suffer from a lack of labour, so workers from the cities, particularly women, were recruited to work on farms. Harpertoun took on some of these 'land girls' who had to learn quickly how to milk the cows and handle horses that were still needed around the farm, despite tractors being available. Fuel rationing meant that the tractors were only used for tasks like ploughing and pulling the various machinery, like harvesters. Later, Italian prisoners were made available to farms. The prisoners lived on the farms and were paid for their work. They were often able to provide skills from their pre-war occupations, such as carpenters and blacksmiths. After the war ended some of the Italian prisoners returned to Britain as migrants, rather than prisoners.

***

By 1944 Jim at Flagstaff had decided to sell the farm and move across to a farm closer to Kelso. He selected a farm of 800 acres, which he purchased for £13,500, at £16 per acre. The farm, called Lurdenlaw, was not really set up for dairying so a new 100 cow byre and dairy had to be constructed. This meant that the cows at Flagstaff could not be brought across straight away, delaying the sale of Flagstaff. So, Jim found himself running two farms at the same time. After the milking had been finished at Flagstaff he would drive across to Kelso in order to supervise work on Lurdenlaw, then he would drive back to Flagstaff in order to milk the cows in the afternoon. This carried on for several months into 1945, until eventually the dairy and byre at Lurdenlaw were ready to take the Flagstaff dairy herd, which was brought across by train. It was an exhausting period of time for Jim, particularly as Maggie was expecting another daughter, Barbara, who was the first of their family to be born at Lurdenlaw.

CHAPTER 20
1947–1965

In the years after the war the Baird family were settled and prospered. Tom, the eldest son, had retired from farming before the war and his son John had taken over Birnieknowe. However, John decided to move operations to England, where the weather was warmer and markets were closer. So, in May 1949, after buying a farm at Andover, the animals, machinery and the family travelled the 450 miles on a train that was dubbed by the local newspapers as the 'Noah's Ark Special'. John's son Tom, or Wilson as he was more commonly known, and his family continued the long Baird farming tradition, that stretched back to the seventeenth century. Elder Tom stayed up in Scotland and spent much time visiting his daughter Bessie, who lived in a house close to Harpertoun, with her husband Tom Houston and sons.

In Canada, Hugh continued on the farm that he had taken back, until Alex came back from his war service. Unfortunately, Alex had suffered a shattered ankle, so it was a little while before he was fit enough to tackle the heavy work around the farm. Hugh and Maggie had travelled over to Scotland a number of times during the inter-war years, to visit family. However, Maggie passed away in 1945, so when Alex had fully taken over the farm, he retired to a cabin that he had built close to the main house, from where he was able to visit his grandchildren and take them to a nearby lake to swim. In 1956 he again travelled across the Atlantic for a five-month visit. In 1960 he was hit by a lorry when crossing a road and died from his injuries a little while later.

Gilbert continued to farm at Glenside with his wife Mary. They never had any more children after the untimely death of John and Agnes in 1932. Gilbert passed away in 1965. While Chrissie and John Todd farmed Polshill for many years, bringing up their family, until John passed away in 1955.

Meanwhile, young Gilbert had taken over the running of Harpertoun from his father. Although John was often seen walking around the farm and offering his opinion on what was taking place. He used to help out cleaning up the dairy after milking and each Saturday he would fill one of the large steel sinks with some of the hot water, which was heated for all the washing that was required. He would then strip off his clothes and immerse himself in the water for his weekly bath. Everyone around the farm knew to avoid the dairy washroom on a Saturday morning, in order that they did not walk in on a naked John Baird! However, it was some months after he started this habit that someone asked him why his hair was looking ginger. John had had white hair for most of his life. It had turned white when he was a young man after he fell ill with a fever. His hair continued to turn ginger over the following weeks, much to the amusement of everyone who met him. He had to sustain a lot of teasing from family and friends. The cause of John's change in hair colour was not fully discovered, however, the water used for all the washing came from a well in a field not far from the dairy, so it was assumed that there were iron salts in this water that was staining the hair. It was probably a blessing that there were not copper salts in the water, otherwise his hair might have turned green.

The Harpertoun family had later taken over the running of another nearby farm called Hassington Mains, so there was a quite a considerable acreage now being farmed, about 1,000 acres. The dairy herd was now one of the biggest in the region and gained a reputation for its high-quality cows, following on from the example set by great uncle Andrew, fifty years previously.

Robert had moved down south and taken over a farm in Gloucestershire, with his new wife Catherine. It was not far from the farm where his sister Mary lived with her husband, Adam Letham. The youngest member of John's family, Flora, married a local man, Mark Craig, and they brought up their family on Wormerlaw Farm, not too far away from Harpertoun.

***

After the Second World War there was a huge rebuilding programme. Cities like London had had large industrial areas and much of its infrastructure destroyed by bombing. As well as rebuilding with better factories and housing, the government were keen to develop new industries and one of these new developments was nuclear power. The site chosen for Britain's first large scale nuclear power plant was thirty-seven miles south of Silloth at a place then called Windscale, but later renamed Sellafield.

On 10 October 1957 a fire started in the main nuclear reactor. The fire caused large amounts of radioactive particles to be released. During the building of the facility the project leader Sir John Cockcroft had become sufficiently concerned about the possibility of radioactive particles being emitted, in the event of exactly such an accident of this type, that he insisted that filters be added to the chimneys that released hot vapours from the reactors. These filters were called Cockcroft's Follies, as most of the nuclear scientists did not share Cockcroft's concerns and belittled the waste of money. However, during the fire the filters stopped 95% of the radioactive particles from leaking into the air around Windscale. Despite the presence of the filters, a significant amount of radioactivity spread across the Lake District. Initially the accident was played down and newspaper reports wrote about a 'minor mishap' having taken place at the Windscale plant. As the extent and possible consequences of the radiation leak became more apparent, tests were carried out on milk produced from local farms and were found to have dangerous levels of radioactivity. Orders were quickly issued for all the milk from 500 km² of to be poured away down drains. This lasted for a month. So, at Wampool Farm John and his workers had to pour away all the milk that they collected each day, while worrying about the milk that they had been drinking and selling prior to the orders being issued. It was estimated that about 100 fatalities have resulted from this radiation leak and others that had occurred before and since the 1957 fire. History now records that Sir John Cockcroft's decision to insist on the installation of the filters in the chimneys averted an international nuclear disaster.

Epilogue

❦

The children of John Baird and Flora Mitchell grew up at Meikle Garclaugh Farm at New Cumnock. Only Tom and John's descendants have continued the Baird farming tradition, with farms around Wigton in Cumbria; Kelso in Roxburghshire; Andover in Hampshire and Cheltenham in Gloucestershire. Hugh's descendants have gone on to a variety of careers in Canada while Chrissie's descendants still live around New Cumnock, although none have stayed in farming. One of Chrissie's grandsons, Andrew Howatt, who has helped with the research for this book, still works as an agricultural engineer. Mary, Andrew, William and Gilbert all passed away without issue.

My grandfather, John James Baird left his birthplace to find his own way in the farming world, armed with a formidable work ethic and a determination to succeed. He first managed a farm in Ayrshire for several years before leasing a farm in Cumberland. From this tenuous start as a tenant farmer, he worked hard to improve the land, breed top quality livestock and grab business opportunities that arose. He probably overstretched his finances at times, but most of the risks that he took succeeded. His family and friends soon began to call him '*the man with the golden hands*' as it seemed to them that every venture that he undertook prospered. He was to help all his children acquire farms of their own and his descendants now farm many thousands of acres, both in Scotland and in England.

He was admired and liked by all those who knew him. At an event held at the White Heather Club near Silloth, one friend sang a song to honour John. Unfortunately, only the first verse has survived.

Do you ken John Baird
With his fine herd of kye,
that he milks in the morn
Afore the sun's in the sky.
He's hard, hard at work
while other folks lie
in their beds on a frosty morning.

In 1957 John and Mary travelled down to the Lake District with their daughter Flora and her husband Mark. On their way back to Kelso they stopped for a rest and John decided to cross the road to look at a field of corn. He waited for a motorbike to pass, but failed to hear or see a second motorbike coming close behind. He was struck by the second motorbike and suffered considerable injuries. He died later in hospital. He was eighty years old.

Fictional characters introduced to help tell the story of the Baird family.

Chapter 1. Marion the dairymaid at Mid-Buiston Farm.
Jack Vass the farm labourer at Mid-Buiston Farm.
Jim the Glaswegian miner who Hugh meets on the ship to Canada.
May, the housemaid at Mid-Buiston Farm.
Sarah Coe, housemaid at Meikle Garclaugh.

Chapter 5. Catherine Wright, a neighbouring farmer to John and Barbara Baird.

Chapter 6. Percy Brown the postman.
George, the farm labourer at Balladoyle farm.
Mary, the maid at Balladoyle.

Chapter 7. Janet Campbell, the housekeeper at Balladoyle.

Chapter 10. Jim Campbell, soldier travelling with Hugh Baird.
Major Anderson, Hugh's commanding officer at Shoreditch.
Andrew Hamilton, soldier at Shoreditch camp with Hugh.
Harry McCauley, soldier at Shoreditch camp with Hugh.
John Robertson, soldier at Shoreditch camp with Hugh.

Chapter 11. Duncan Wilson, neighbouring farmer to Balladoyle.
Tom, friend of Allan Stevenson who fires the rifle and kills Allan.

Chapter 13. Agnes, maid at Meikle Garclaugh Farm.

Chapter 14. Edward, Hugh Baird's farm labourer at Mansfield farm, Canada.
Edward Anderson, milk cooperative partner with John Baird.

Chapter 15. Janet, a dairymaid at Balladoyle.

Appendix

ⲉⲁⲇⲟ

2nd June 1920

THE LATE MR ANDREW M. BAIRD GARCLAUGH

The decease of Mr Baird on Saturday last at the early age of forty-seven years leaves a big blank in the ranks of Ayrshire stock-breeders. For a very long period of years the Garclaugh herd has been famous wherever the Ayrshire cow is known, and Mr Baird, from his youth onwards, was a notable figure in the actual world. The herd was brought from a high state of perfection by his father, the late Mr John Baird, and on his death many years ago his son went on year after year adding to its quality.

Quite a score of years ago, Mr Andrew Baird saw great possibilities opening up in the export trade, and went strongly into that lucrative line. Thus, the Garclaugh strain has gone all over the world to improve the qualities of deep-milking cows in many wide-scattered lands. The Continent, United States and Canada, South Africa and Japan can all show the great results of the Garclaugh blood. One record milking cow, the great May Mischief, swept the showyards of the States and left a glorious stock behind her. The great feeding stuff manufacturing firms were proud to secure o'clock order, for it meant a splendid testimonial to them, which they used well.

Sterling methods marked the secret of Mr Baird's success. Constant grading up was the object of his life. He fixed a type of cow beautiful in all its points, and at the same time a cow that set the foaming luggie running over. His masterful selection of stock bulls from a great area concentrated all the best Ayrshire blood in the Garclaugh herd, which he graded up and raised year by year until it is now second to none.

When milk records came on the scene, Mr Baird was ready, and a good track record was household property whenever there was a byre.

Then came the boom in Ayrshire bulls that still rages on. Once more Mr Baird was ready. For some years the annual Garclaugh draft was the feature of the sale ring. This spring he resolved to sell at home, and the result amply justified the step, for the sale realised the handsome average of £94.

That sale was his last triumph. For a considerable time past his health had been very unsatisfactory. He was unable to be out of doors that day, and his many friends saw, to their infinite regret, that the sale would be his last. He carried on gallantly, working steadily after all hope was gone, right up to the end, which came last Saturday.

Mr Baird was a good, cheery companion, his life was pleasing and simple. His herd and his farm got all the benefits of his devoted enthusiasm and splendid skill with stock, and they were sufficient for him. Public life had little traction for his retiring nature, and he took a little part in it. He was unmarried, and the greatest sympathy is expressed for his aged mother in her sorrow.

15th February 1922

THE LATE MRS BAIRD, GARCLAUGH

Mrs Baird, approaching four-score, closed to a long and eminently useful career. None was better known, and no one could be more respected in all the farming community then she. Come of Ayrshire farming stock, she was an honour to the race she sprang from. A fine type of the old Scotswoman, she played her part well. Of late, trouble has laid a heavy hand on her, and one break after another in her family had heaped sorrow upon sorrow. For a good long time past it was plain that she was failing, and the winter was sore on her. She passed peacefully away at last, mourned by all the wide circle who knew her.

THE LATE MR JOHN BAIRD, HARPERTOUN

I have been unable to locate an obituary for my grandfather, John James Baird. If any member of the Baird family knows where I can find an obituary then I would be grateful, to receive a copy.

Signing up or attestation papers for Gilbert Baird when he joined the Canadian Army

174th Batt'n. C.E.F. (Cameron Highlanders of Canada)

ATTESTATION - PAPER.

No. 593151

Folio.

CANADIAN OVER-SEAS EXPEDITIONARY FORCE.

QUESTIONS TO BE PUT BEFORE ATTESTATION.
(ANSWERS.)

1. What is your surname? ... BAIRD.
1a. What are your Christian names? ... Gilbert.
1b. What is your present address? ... McAuley, Man.
2. In what Town, Township or Parish, and in what Country were you born? ... New Cumnock, Ayrshire, Scotland.
3. What is the name of your next of kin? ... Mrs. John Baird.
4. What is the address of your next-of-kin? ... New Cumnock, Ayrshire, Scotland.
4a. What is the relationship of your next-of-kin? ... Mother.
5. What is the date of your birth? ... August 11th. 1896.
6. What is your Trade or Calling? ... Farmer
7. Are you married? ... No.
8. Are you willing to be vaccinated or re-vaccinated and inoculated? ... Yes.
9. Do you now belong to the Active Militia? ... Yes.
10. Have you ever served in any Military Force?. If so, state particulars of former Service. ... Yes. 79th. C.H. of C. No.
11. Do you understand the nature and terms of your engagement? ... Yes.
12. Are you willing to be attested to serve in the CANADIAN OVER-SEAS EXPEDITIONARY FORCE? ... Yes.

DECLARATION TO BE MADE BY MAN ON ATTESTATION.

I, ..., do solemnly declare that the above are answers made by me to the above questions and that they are true, and that I am willing to fulfil the engagements by me now made, and I hereby engage and agree to serve in the Canadian Over-Seas Expeditionary Force, and to be attached to any arm of the service therein, for the term of one year, or during the war now existing between Great Britain and Germany should that war last longer than one year, and for six months after the termination of that war provided His Majesty should so long require my services, or until legally discharged.

Gilbert Baird (Signature of Recruit)

Date September 6th. 1916. _H. Gardiner_ (Signature of Witness)

OATH TO BE TAKEN BY MAN ON ATTESTATION.

I, ..., do make Oath, that I will be faithful and bear true Allegiance to His Majesty King George the Fifth, His Heirs and Successors, and that I will as in duty bound honestly and faithfully defend His Majesty, His Heirs and Successors, in Person, Crown and Dignity, against all enemies, and will observe and obey all orders of His Majesty, His Heirs and Successors, and of all the Generals and Officers set over me. So help me God.

Gilbert Baird (Signature of Recruit)

Date September 6th. 1916. _H. Gardiner_ (Signature of Witness)

CERTIFICATE OF MAGISTRATE.

The Recruit above-named was cautioned by me that if he made any false answer to any of the above questions he would be liable to be punished as provided in the Army Act.

The above questions were then read to the Recruit in my presence.

I have taken care that he understands each question, and that his answer to each question has been duly entered as replied to, and the said Recruit has made and signed the declaration and taken the oath before me, at McAuley, Man. this 6th. day of September 1916.

J. A. Keachen (Signature of Justice) J.P.

M. F. W. 23
750M—8-15
N. Q. 1773-40-341

I WISH TO MARK, BY THIS PERSONAL MESSAGE, my appreciation of the service you have rendered to your Country in 1939.

In the early days of the War you opened your door to strangers who were in need of shelter, & offered to share your home with them.

I know that to this unselfish task you have sacrificed much of your own comfort, & that it could not have been achieved without the loyal co-operation of all in your household.

By your sympathy you have earned the gratitude of those to whom you have shown hospitality, & by your readiness to serve you have helped the State in a work of great value—

Elizabeth R

J. Baird, Esq.,
Harpertoun.

www.ingramcontent.com/pod-product-compliance
Lightning Source LLC
Chambersburg PA
CBHW072038080426
42733CB00010B/1934